common core

Performance Coach™

③

English Language Arts

Performance Coach, English Language Arts, Grade 3   334NASE   ISBN-13: 978-1-62362-841-3   B
Cover Image: © Thinkstock

Triumph Learning® 136 Madison Avenue, 7th Floor, New York, NY 10016

CONTENTS

Standards

Standards

W.3.1.a–d, W.3.2.a–d, W.3.3.a,
W.3.3.c, W.3.3.d, W.3.4, W.3.5, L.3.1.h

W.3.1.a–d, L.3.1.e

W.3.3.a–d, L.3.2.c

W.3.6, W.3.7, W.3.8, L.3.2.a

W.3.2.a–d, L.3.1.i

W.3.1.a–d, L.3.1.f

W.3.5, L.3.1.a, L.3.1.d–i, L.3.2.a–g,
L.3.3.a

SL.3.2, L.3.4.d

SL.3.2, SL.3.3, L.3.1.g

DEAR STUDENT

Welcome to *Performance Coach*!

We made this book to help you strengthen your reading, writing, and listening skills. These skills are important to have for every subject you study this year, not just English Language Arts.

Each lesson in this book has three parts:

GETTING THE IDEA ①

Review some of the basic concepts and skills you've already learned.

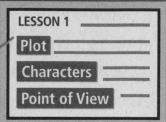

② COACHED EXAMPLE

Read a passage or two, then answer a set of questions. Don't worry—the questions have hints that will help you!

LESSON PRACTICE ③

Now you're on your own! This part contains a longer passage and additional questions to answer.

There are many different types of test items in *Performance Coach*. For some, you will have to choose more than one answer. For others, you will write out your answer. You will also see items that ask you to match words and phrases, put events in order, or complete a graphic organizer. Many items have more than one part. Be sure to read the directions carefully so you know how to answer each item.

HAVE A GREAT YEAR!

Sincerely,
TRIUMPH LEARNING

STRAND 1

Working with Literature

RL.3.1, RL.3.2, RL.3.3, RL.3.5, RL.3.6, RL.3.7, L.3.4.a

Fiction

① GETTING THE IDEA

You have probably listened to or read stories that were made up. Stories made up by people are called **fiction**. Some fiction stories are short—just a few pages. Other fiction stories are whole books. The books may be broken up into chapters.

There are many kinds of fiction. Look at the chart below. How many kinds of fiction have you read? What parts of the story helped you know what kind of fiction it was?

Kind of Fiction	Definition
present-day fiction	a story that takes place in the present time
historical fiction	a story that takes place in the past and may tell about important people or events from history
science fiction	a story that tells about science, machines, and events of the future; it may take place in other worlds
folktale	a story that is passed down from one person to another over time; fables and myths are both types of folktales
fable	a story that teaches a lesson; it usually has animal characters who act as people sometimes do
myth	a story that explains how things in nature came to be; it may also tell how and why things work the way they do

Every piece of fiction has the following parts: characters, a setting, a plot, a theme, and a point of view.

Characters

Characters in a story can be people, animals, or even objects. You can learn about characters from what they say and do, and from what other characters say about them.

Read this paragraph. Underline the words that show why nobody liked Jason.

> Nobody on the baseball team liked Jason. He bragged that he was better than anyone else. He made fun of other players when they struck out.

Setting

The **setting** is where and when a story takes place. The setting may be in our world or a made-up place. It may be in the past, present, or future. Underline the words that tell the setting of this paragraph.

> The noon sun blazed in the sky. The dinosaurs were searching for water on the open grassland. Then, dark clouds appeared, and raindrops began to fall.

Plot

A story is made up of **events**, or things that happen. The order of events in a story is called the **plot**. Each character takes actions that cause events to happen.

Read the sentences below. What does Anna want? How do her actions lead to a new event?

> Anna was determined to be an artist. She practiced drawing every day and won a contest to go to art camp. At art camp, she met a new friend named Pradeep.

Illustrations

Illustrations are drawings that help you understand a story. They may show what the characters, setting, and events look like. They can show the mood of the story or of the characters. These pictures may make you feel happy, sad, or even frightened.

Theme

The **theme** of a story is the lesson or central message that the writer wants to share. "Be careful what you wish for" and "Good deeds are often rewarded" are two themes. Each is a lesson about life that the characters might learn.

Point of View

Everyone has a **point of view**, or a way of looking at the world. A story is told from the point of view of a **narrator**. A narrator may be a character or someone outside the story.

The reader may agree or disagree with the narrator's opinions. For example, suppose a story is narrated by a character who thinks he is being punished unfairly. You, as a reader, may think the punishment is fair, based on the character's actions.

Read this paragraph. Underline the words that tell the narrator's opinion of the third little pig. Do you agree or disagree with the narrator? Why?

> The first little pig built a house of straw. The wolf blew it down. The second little pig built a house of wood. The wolf knocked it down. The third little pig was the smartest one of all. He built his house of brick, and the wolf could not destroy it.

Language Spotlight • Context Clues

If you come to a word you don't know when you are reading, look at other words in the sentences nearby. These nearby words are called **context clues**. They can help you figure out the meaning of an unknown word.

Read the sentences below. Underline words that are clues to the meaning of *heron*.

> Ava stared at the heron as it splashed in the pond. It moved through the water on long, thin legs. When it saw Ava, it spread its big wings and flew away into the bushes.

Read the passage.

The Fox and the Crow

adapted from a fable by Aesop

A fox once saw a crow fly off with a piece of cheese in its beak. The crow landed on the branch of a nearby tree.

That cheese looks so delicious. I'm going to get it away from that silly crow, thought the fox. He quickly made a plan. Then he walked up to the foot of the tree.

"Good day, Mr. Crow," he said politely. "You are looking very handsome today. Your feathers are very shiny, and your eyes are quite bright."

"Thank you, sir," said the crow. "You are looking very well yourself."

The fox continued with his plan. He said, "I have heard that you have a beautiful voice. In fact, I was told that you sing better than any other crow. Would you sing just one song for me?"

The crow lifted up his head and began to sing. Like all crows, he could only let out a rough *caw*. But the minute the crow opened his mouth, the piece of cheese fell to the ground.

The fox snapped up the lump of cheese. After gulping it down, he looked up at the angry crow.

"Well, you were easy to trick!" said the fox. "All I wanted was that piece of cheese. To pay you back, I will give you a piece of good advice. Don't ever trust anyone who <u>flatters</u> you."

Answer the following questions.

1 How does the illustration give you a better idea of the story's events?

A. It shows that the fox is ready to grab the cheese.

B. It shows how angry the fox is at the crow.

C. It shows that the fox is smaller than the crow.

D. It shows how the fox climbs up the tree.

Hint Look carefully at the picture. Which part of the story does it show? As you read each choice above, think about the one that relates to an important event in the story.

2 These events are from the story, but they are out of order. Write the numbers 2, 3, 4, 5, or 6 to put the events in the correct order.

1	The crow flies to a tree with cheese in his beak.
	The fox asks the crow to sing.
	The fox eats the cheese.
	The fox tells the crow that he has a beautiful voice.
	The crow opens his mouth to sing and drops the cheese.
	The fox makes a plan to get the cheese.
7	The fox gives the crow advice.

Hint To put the events in order, think about how the events build on one another. How does one event cause the next one to happen?

3 At the end of the story, the fox says, "Don't ever trust anyone who <u>flatters</u> you." Use the context clues underlined in the sentences below to explain what it means to flatter someone.

> **"You are looking <u>very handsome</u> today. Your feathers are <u>very shiny</u>, and your eyes are <u>quite bright</u>."**
>
> **"Well, you were easy to <u>trick</u>!" said the fox.**

_____

_____

_____

> **Hint** To find the meaning of *flatter*, look back at the sentences that show how the fox talks about the crow. Do you think the fox truly admires the crow?

4 The following question has two parts. First, answer Part A. Then, answer Part B.

Part A

What is the lesson of the story?

A. People should share food with friends.

B. Be careful about whom you believe.

C. Think about what you are going to do before you act.

D. Tricky people will be punished in the end.

Part B

Which sentence from the story **best** supports your answer to Part A?

A. "That cheese looks so delicious."

B. "Good day, Mr. Crow," he said politely.

C. "Would you sing just one song for me?"

D. "Don't ever trust anyone who flatters you."

> **Hint** The lesson in a fable is usually stated by a character or by the narrator. Who states the lesson in this fable?

Use the Reading Guide to help you understand the passage.

Auac and Lamiran

adapted from a Filipino fable, retold by Dean S. Fansler

Reading Guide

What details help you picture the setting of this story?

What traits do you learn about Lamarin in this section? What does the narrator tell you about Lamarin's character?

What is Lamiran's goal?

Long ago, a cluster of islands basked in the sun of the South China Sea. Today these islands are known as the Philippines, but back when they were new, they had no name. Their jungles were full of fruit trees, and their glittering waters were full of fish. The islands were home to hundreds of animals and also some people. Most of the people were farmers or fishermen. They rose early to work long, hard days in their rice fields and fishing boats.

Some of the animals helped the farmers. The roosters crowed to wake them up. The water buffalos pulled plows through the water-filled rice fields. But the other animals weren't such hard workers. Instead, they spent their lazy days playing tricks on one another.

One day, a hawk named Auac stole a salted fish. The fish had been hanging in the sun to dry near a fisherman's cottage. The hawk flew with his meal to a branch of a tree. He sat on the branch. Then, he began to eat the delicious fish.

As he was eating, a squirrel named Lamiran came out of a hole in the same tree. The squirrel looked up at the branch. He spotted the hawk eating the fish.

Lamiran was a sneaky fellow. He knew how to use sweet words to get what he wanted. And what he wanted now was Auac's tasty fish. But he wondered how he could get the hawk to drop the fish.

What details in this story remind you of "The Fox and the Crow"?

How does the squirrel get the hawk to drop his fish?

What does the heron advise the hawk to do in the future?

After a while, Lamiran knew what to do. He looked up at the hawk and smiled. "What beautiful shiny black feathers you have!"

When the bird heard this praise, he felt very pleased. He <u>fluttered</u> his wings to show off his feathers. He was indeed happy to be admired.

Lamiran then said, "You are especially beautiful when you walk. You are as graceful on the ground as you are in the air."

Auac did not understand the trick the squirrel was playing on him. He hopped along the branch with the <u>air</u> of a king. But his hopping was not very graceful.

The clever squirrel went on <u>praising</u> the hawk. "I heard someone say yesterday that your voice was soft and lovely. Everyone who listens to your song is delighted. Please sing for me!" said the squirrel.

Auac felt prouder than ever. He opened his mouth and sang, "Uwk-uwk-uwk!" As he made his loud, ugly noises, the fish dropped and fell to the ground. Lamiran leaped on it and ran away.

In a nearby stream, a heron and a water buffalo were watching. The heron lifted his long beak from the water and shook his feathered head. He said, "Auac, let me give you some advice. You shouldn't always believe what others tell you. Think for yourself!"

The water buffalo shook his horns as if to say, "Don't make that mistake again!"

Answer the following questions.

1 Read the sentences on the left. Match each underlined word to its closest meaning on the right.

A. He <u>fluttered</u> his wings to show off his feathers.

B. He hopped along the branch with the <u>air</u> of a king.

C. The clever squirrel went on <u>praising</u> the hawk. "I heard someone say yesterday that your voice was soft and lovely."

1. say admiring words about someone or something

2. the way someone acts

3. wave or flap very fast

2 The following question has two parts. First, answer Part A. Then, answer Part B.

Part A

How does the squirrel know that the hawk can be fooled?

A. The squirrel sees that the hawk is not going to eat all of the fish.

B. The heron tells the squirrel that the hawk is foolish.

C. The hawk accepts the squirrel's praise without thinking.

D. The hawk is not graceful as he hops along the branch.

Part B

Underline **two** sentences in the story that support your answer to Part A.

3 The hawk and the heron are very different characters. How might the story have been different if it were told from the heron's point of view?

_____

_____

_____

_____

4 Which statement below **best** explains what the heron means when he says to the hawk, "Think for yourself"?

A. Ask someone you trust when you are not sure what is true or false.

B. Be careful about who you make friends with.

C. Listen to what others say, or you'll be sorry.

D. Form your own opinions, and don't just believe what others say.

5 The following question has two parts. First, answer Part A. Then, answer Part B.

Part A

Which word **best** describes Lamiran, the squirrel?

A. helpful

B. lively

C. clever

D. thoughtful

Part B

Write **two** sentences from the story that support your answer to Part A.

_____

_____

_____

_____

_____

Characters

Like other stories, a drama has characters. The characters in a drama are called the **cast**. A list of the cast is included at the beginning of the play. It is called the **cast of characters**. In a drama, the character names are shown in all capital letters. Read this cast of characters. How many characters are in this cast?

> **Cast of Characters**
>
> MS. LOPEZ, a teacher
>
> LAYLA, a student
>
> BILLY, a new student

Dialogue

The characters in a play do a lot of talking. In fact, almost the whole story is told through dialogue. The words the characters say are called **dialogue**. Dialogue helps you learn what the characters feel and think.

The dialogue in a play looks different from dialogue in a story. It does not have quotation marks around it. The words the characters speak come after their names. Which words are spoken in the example below?

> MS. LOPEZ: Layla, this is Billy. Billy just moved here.
>
> LAYLA: (*shakes Billy's hand*) Hi, Billy. How do you like our school so far?
>
> BILLY: It's a lot bigger than my old school. (*sighs*) I hope I don't get lost.
>
> LAYLA: Don't worry. I'll help you. Everyone will. I know because I was a new student last year!

Stage Directions

Look at the example again. The words in italic type inside the parentheses ( ) are stage directions. **Stage directions** give instructions to the actors on how to say dialogue and how to move. In the example, what should Layla do when she says "Hi" to Billy? What does Billy do when he answers Layla?

Stage directions also tell about lighting and sound or props and costumes. Props are the things the characters use in a play. Costumes are any special clothes they wear.

Theme

Just like fiction stories, a drama has a theme. The **theme** is the central message or lesson about life that the author wants the audience to learn. An example of a theme is "Be kind to others." Think about what the characters do and say, how they respond to one another, and what they learn from their experiences to help you figure out the theme.

Putting It All Together

When you watch a drama, you see and hear everything that happens. When you read a drama, you have to pay attention to all the parts to understand what happens. As you read, try to picture the play in your mind.

Language Spotlight • Root Words and Affixes

An **affix** is a word part added to the beginning or end of a root word. A **root word** is the base, or main part, of a word. An affix added to the beginning of a root word is called a **prefix**. An affix added to the end of a root word is called a **suffix**.

Read these examples. Complete the last two words in the chart. Each has two affixes.

Word	Prefix or Suffix	Root Word
preview	pre-	view
spotless	-less	spot
sunny	-y	sun
disagreeable	dis-, -able	agree
uncomfortable		
replacement		

Read the play.

Food Fun

Cast of Characters

SAM, a third-grade boy
FIONA, Sam's friend and classmate
REBECCA, Sam's sister, a fourth-grade girl

Act I, Scene 1

Setting: Present-day school cafeteria. It's lunchtime, and Sam, Rebecca, and Fiona are at the end of a line, holding empty trays. Two or three students are ahead of them. Several students are seated, eating lunch.

SAM: (*nudges Fiona*) Hey, Fi, do you know why the bacon laughed at the egg?

REBECCA: (*groans*) Oh no, Sam. You're not going to tell the jokes you told at dinner last night! They were so . . . *un*funny.

FIONA: (*nods at Sam*) Go on, Sam. Why? Why did the bacon laugh?

(*The children move forward in the line.*)

SAM: The egg cracked a yolk. Get it? *Joke* and *yolk* sound alike.

REBECCA: (*groans*) It's not funny if you have to explain it, Sam.

FIONA: (*laughs*) Tell another one, Sam!

(*The children move forward in the line.*)

SAM: (*makes a face at Rebecca*) Sure thing, Fi. What's the best thing to put into a pie?

FIONA: I don't know. What *is* the best thing to put into a pie?

SAM: Your fork!

REBECCA: (*groans, but smiles*) See, Fiona. I told you they were bad!

FIONA: (*laughs*) That's part of the reason they're so funny. Tell another, Sam.

(*The children move to the lunch counter.*)

SAM: Let's get our food first, Fi.

Act I, Scene 2

A few minutes later. Sam, Fiona, and Rebecca are now seated at a lunch table.

FIONA: OK, Sam. Another joke.

REBECCA: No, please! (*picks up sandwich*) You're going to ruin my appetite.

SAM: (*winks at Fiona*) OK, Fi. Here's a knock-knock joke. (*sips his milk*) Knock, knock.

FIONA: Who's there?

SAM: Lettuce.

FIONA: Lettuce who?

SAM: Let-us eat!

FIONA: (*laughs*) You have to admit that that one was funny, Rebecca!

REBECCA: (*covers a smile*) It was funny the *first* time I heard it. But these jokes are just a rerun of last night. (*puts down sandwich*) Here's a new one. Knock, knock.

SAM: (*looks puzzled*) Who's there?

REBECCA: Eggs.

SAM: Eggs who?

REBECCA: (*smiles*) *Eggs*-cuse me as I make an *eggs*-it. I'll eat with my other friends, so Fiona can enjoy the rest of your jokes! (*rises, picks up tray*) I'll see you two later.

(*Rebecca moves to another table. Curtain closes.*)

Answer the following questions.

1 Read the examples from the play on the left. Then, match each example with the description of it on the right.

A. SAM, a third-grade boy
FIONA, Sam's friend and classmate

1. dialogue

2. setting

B. *Present-day school cafeteria.*

3. stage direction

C. (*winks at Fiona*)

D. FIONA: Who's there?

4. characters

Hint Think about the way the different parts of drama are shown in a play.

2 *Food Fun* is a one-act play with two scenes. How does the setting change from Scene 1 to Scene 2?

Write your answer on the lines below.

_____

_____

_____

Hint The setting is where and when a story takes place. What is different about the setting in Scene 2?

3 The following question has two parts. First, answer Part A. Then, answer Part B.

Part A

Read these sentences from the play and the directions that follow.

It was funny the *first* time I heard it. But these jokes are just a rerun of last night.

Which **two** words have an affix in them?

A. night

B. rerun

C. funny

D. heard

Part B

Write the root word and affix for each word you chose in Part A.

_____

Hint An affix is a word part added to a root word. A prefix comes at the beginning of the word, and a suffix comes at the end. Look for affixes and root words to answer Part A. Then, answer Part B.

4 How can you tell that Rebecca thinks Sam's jokes are funny even though she says they are not?

Write your answer on the lines below.

_____

_____

_____

Hint Look back at the play. Read Rebecca's dialogue and look at the stage directions that tell how she should act. How a character acts can tell you how he or she really feels.

Use the Reading Guide to help you understand the drama.

The Man and the Alligator

adapted from a Honduran folktale,
retold by Augusta Stevenson

Reading Guide

Where does Scene 1 take place? How does the setting change in Scene 2?

What favor does Man do for Alligator?

Remember to think about what the characters say and do to figure out what they are like.

Cast of Characters

MAN

ALLIGATOR, in costume

WOLF, in costume

LEOPARD, in costume

RABBIT, in costume

"The Man and the Alligator" is a one-act play with two scenes. In Scene 1, a man finds an alligator in his garden after a storm. The alligator is hurt and asks the man to carry him back to the river. The alligator promises to return the favor and help the man in the future. Read what happens in Scene 2 below.

Act I, Scene 2

Setting: Afternoon of the same day. Riverbank. Man enters, dragging Alligator in a net.

MAN: Here we are, Brother Alligator. (*unties net*)

ALLIGATOR: (*crawls out of net*) Thank you. But I'm still hungry and weak. Please help me down to the water.

MAN: (*helps Alligator to river bank*) You should be fine now. I'll leave you now.

ALLIGATOR: (*grabs the Man's leg*) No!

MAN: (*alarmed*) Let go of my leg! You're hurting me!

ALLIGATOR: No, I won't. (*slowly*) I—am—going—to—eat—you.

MAN: Eat me? Is that the way you repay a favor, by doing a wrong?

What problem does Man have? How does he try to solve the problem?

What do Wolf and Leopard mean when they say they would repay someone who has done them a favor "by doing him a wrong"?

ALLIGATOR: (*hisses*) That's the way of all animals. None of us will remember a favor or a friend when we are hungry.

MAN: (*tugs at leg*) I won't believe that. Let's ask the first animal that comes to the river to drink. (*Wolf enters and goes to the riverbank.*) Wolf, tell me. How would you repay someone who has done you a favor?

WOLF: By doing him a wrong. (*drinks and exits*)

ALLIGATOR: (*laughs*) Just as I said! Now I shall eat you!

MAN: (*begs*) No, please. Let us ask another. (*Leopard enters and goes to the riverbank.*) Leopard, tell me. How do you repay someone who has done you a favor?

LEOPARD: By doing him a wrong. (*drinks and exits*)

ALLIGATOR: (*laughs*) See? Just as I told you. Now I shall eat you.

MAN: (*shouts*) Help! Help!

(*Rabbit enters*)

RABBIT: Oh, hello, Ally. Whom are you about to eat?

ALLIGATOR: I am about to eat a man.

MAN: (*interrupts*) Brother Rabbit, how do you repay a favor?

RABBIT: Hello, Man. Why do you ask?

MAN: Just this morning, Alligator was in my garden. He destroyed my garden—

ALLIGATOR: (*interrupts*) I was blown there by the storm!

MAN: (*continues*) Alligator was hurt. He begged me to carry him to the river. He promised to return the favor if I helped him. Now, he wants to eat me!

Why does Rabbit act surprised when Man says he carried Alligator in his net?

How do the stage directions help you understand what Alligator does to prove that he can fit in the net?

What does Rabbit say and do to change things for Man and the Alligator?

RABBIT: But Man, how did you bring Alligator here?

MAN: I carried him in my net.

RABBIT: (*surprised*) No! Ally, you couldn't possibly fit in that small net. It's <u>unbelievable</u>.

ALLIGATOR: (*angrily*) It's true! You don't believe it? Well, I can prove it to you. (*turning to Man*) Get your net, and we'll show Rabbit how it was done. (*Man gets net and opens it.*) First, I crawl inside like this. (*crawls into net*) Then, I curl up like this. (*curls up in net*) See? I fit!

RABBIT: I see! But the net is quite open. You'd fall out if Man dragged you.

ALLIGATOR: Man, show Rabbit how you tied the net.

MAN: (*ties net*) I tied it just like this, Brother Rabbit.

RABBIT: (*checks knot*) Yes, it looks quite tight. Why, Ally, you can hardly move!

ALLIGATOR: You're right, Rabbit. I can't.

RABBIT: Well, Brother Man, now that you have him, don't let him go.

ALLIGATOR: (*surprised*) What?

MAN: (*to Rabbit*) I won't. Thank you, Brother Rabbit, for helping me.

RABBIT: No thanks are needed. I remembered the turnips you gave me last winter when the ground was covered with snow. Some animals *do* return a favor.

Answer the following questions.

1 How is the play *The Man and the Alligator* different from a story? Choose **all** that apply.

   A. The characters include people and animals.

   B. There is a cast of characters that lists the cast.

   C. It is divided into parts called acts and scenes.

   D. It is divided into parts called chapters.

   E. The characters' names are in all capital letters.

   F. The dialogue has quotation marks.

   G. The dialogue comes after the characters' names.

   H. It has stage directions.

2 Read both parts of the question before responding.

Part A

Read these lines from the play.

> **RABBIT: (*surprised*) No! Ally, you couldn't possibly fit in that small net. It's unbelievable.**

> **ALLIGATOR: (*angrily*) It's true! You don't believe it? Well, I can prove it to you.**

What does the word unbelievable mean?

   A. not able to be believed   **C.** able to believe

   B. believing what you see   **D.** believing what you cannot see

Part B

Which affixes help you figure out the meaning of the word unbelievable?

   A. the affixes *un-* and *-le*   **C.** the affixes *un-* and *-able*

   B. the affixes *be-* and *-able*   **D.** the affixes *re-* and *-le*

3 The following question has two parts. First, answer Part A. Then, answer Part B.

Part A

Read the dialogue from the play and the questions that follow.

> **ALLIGATOR: (*hisses*) That's the way of all animals. None of us will remember a favor or a friend when we are hungry.**

What does Alligator mean when he makes this comment to Man?

_____

_____

Part B

What does Man do to try to prove that Alligator is wrong?

_____

_____

4 The following are events from the play. In each box, write the number 2, 3, 4, or 5 so that the events are in the correct order.

1	A man helps a hurt alligator back to the river.
	A rabbit tricks the alligator into getting back into the man's net.
	The alligator grabs the man's leg and tries to eat him.
	Both the wolf and the leopard say they would do a wrong.
	The man asks a wolf and a leopard how they would return a favor.
6	The rabbit tells the man that he has returned a favor the man did for him.

5 Think about the characters in *The Man and the Alligator* to complete the chart.

Write a word to describe each character, and then tell what the character does or says to show this. One has been done for you.

Character	Description of the Character	What the Character Does or Says to Show This
Man	kind	Man carries Alligator to the river. Man also helped Rabbit in winter.
Alligator		
Rabbit		

6 Think about the lesson the author of the play wants an audience to learn. What do you think the theme or message of the play is?

Remember to use evidence from the text to support your answer.

Write your answer on the lines below.

_____

_____

_____

_____

_____

_____

_____

_____

_____

_____

_____

_____

_____

_____

_____

RL.3.1, RL.3.2, RL.3.3, RL.3.4, RL.3.9, L.3.4.c

Analyze Literature

1 GETTING THE IDEA

When you **analyze** literature, you look more closely at a story, poem, or play you have read. Sometimes you may analyze one text in depth. Other times you may analyze two related texts. When you analyze two texts, look for connections between them. You can compare and contrast the characters, settings, or themes. When you **compare** texts, you look at ways they are alike. When you **contrast** texts, you look at ways they are different.

Recount the Stories

Start by recounting what you remember about each story. When you **recount** stories, you retell what you have read. Describe story parts such as the setting, characters, plot, and theme. Recounting the two stories helps you review them. Then, you can compare and contrast their parts.

Compare and Contrast Plots

The **plot** is what happens in a story. To compare plots, tell what happens in the beginning, middle, and end of each story. Be sure to tell what problem the characters have in each story. How are the problems alike and different? How do the characters solve them? Use a chart like the one below to help you compare and contrast.

	Story 1	Story 2
Beginning		
Middle		
End		
Problem		
Solution		

Compare and Contrast Characters

Characters from two different stories may be alike in some ways. Sometimes, two stories may even share the same characters. To compare characters, look at what each one says and does. What do these words and actions tell you about how the characters are alike and different?

Compare and Contrast Settings

Two stories may have similar or different settings. The **setting** is the place and time of a story. To compare place, look for details in each story about the location, such as in a town or on a farm. To compare time, look at how characters dress and speak. Do they dress and speak like you, or do they dress and speak in an old-fashioned way?

Compare and Contrast Themes

The **theme** is the story's central message. It often isn't told, but the story's events give clues about it. Two stories may have different themes. Or, two stories may have the same theme, even if they have different plots, settings, and characters.

Read each paragraph below. Each one tells the plot of a story. As you read, figure out the theme of each story.

> A lion caught a mouse and was about to eat her. The mouse told the lion that if he let her go, she might be able to help him someday. The lion laughed at the idea that a tiny mouse could help him, but he let her go. Later, the lion got caught in a hunter's net. The mouse chewed through the net to free him.
>
> Jim was playing kickball with his friends when his little brother Ian asked to play. Jim said Ian would just get in the way. Then, Jim accidentally kicked the ball under a fence. Jim and his friends couldn't fit under the fence, but Ian was small enough to fit and get the ball. Ian saved the game.

These two stories have the same theme: Don't be quick to judge people—they may surprise you with what they can do!

Compare and Contrast Points of View

When you compare the **points of view** of two stories, you look at who is telling each one. Is the narrator a character or someone outside the story? To find out, look at whether the person telling the story uses the word *I*. Note whose thoughts and feelings you hear about.

Comparing and Contrasting Checklist

Here are some questions to ask yourself about each story as you begin to compare and contrast them:

- Who are the main characters? What are they like?

- Who is telling the story? Which characters' thoughts and feelings does the narrator tell about?

- What is the setting?

- What is the plot? What happens in the beginning, middle, and end of the story?

- What problem do the characters have? How do they solve it?

- What is the theme or central message?

Language Spotlight • Root Words

When you see a word you don't know, you may be able to figure it out by looking at its root word. A **root word** is the base, or main part, of a word. The same root word can appear in many different words. If you know what it means in one word, you may be able to use it to figure out another.

Look at the examples below. Each underlined word has the same root word: *use*. Using what you know about the word *use*, write down a meaning for each underlined word.

The book had many <u>useful</u> facts.

This broken tool is <u>useless</u>.

You can <u>reuse</u> this lunch bag.

There is no writing in the <u>unused</u> notebook.

Read the passage.

excerpted and adapted from

The Tale of Peter Rabbit

by Beatrix Potter

Once upon a time there were four little Rabbits, and their names were Flopsy, Mopsy, Cotton-tail, and Peter.

They lived with their Mother in a sand-bank, <u>underneath</u> the root of a very big fir-tree.

"Now my dears," said old Mrs. Rabbit one morning, "you may go into the fields or down the lane, but don't go into Mr. McGregor's garden. Your Father had an accident there. He was put in a pie by Mrs. McGregor. Now run along, and don't get into mischief. I am going out."

Then old Mrs. Rabbit took a basket and her umbrella, and went through the wood to the baker's. She bought a loaf of brown bread and five currant buns.

Flopsy, Mopsy, and Cotton-tail, who were good little bunnies, went down the lane to gather blackberries.

But Peter, who was very naughty, ran straight away to Mr. McGregor's garden, and squeezed under the gate!

First he ate some lettuces and some French beans. And then he ate some radishes.

And then, feeling rather sick, he went to look for some parsley.

But round the end of a cucumber frame, whom should he meet but Mr. McGregor!

Mr. McGregor was on his hands and knees planting out young cabbages. But he jumped up and ran after Peter, waving a rake and calling out, "Stop thief!"

Peter was most dreadfully frightened. He rushed all over the garden, for he had forgotten the way back to the gate.

He lost one of his shoes among the cabbages, and the other shoe amongst the potatoes.

After losing them, he ran on four legs and went faster. I think he might have got away altogether if he had not unfortunately run into a gooseberry net, and got caught by the large buttons on his jacket. It was a blue jacket with brass buttons, quite new.

Peter gave himself up for lost, and shed big tears. . . .

Mr. McGregor came up with a sieve, which he intended to pop upon the top of Peter. But Peter wriggled out just in time, leaving his jacket behind him.

He rushed into the tool-shed, and jumped into a can. It would have been a beautiful thing to hide in, if it had not had so much water in it.

Mr. McGregor was quite sure that Peter was somewhere in the tool-shed, perhaps hidden underneath a flower-pot. He began to turn them over carefully, looking under each.

Presently Peter sneezed—"Kertyschoo!" Mr. McGregor was after him in no time.

He tried to put his foot upon Peter, who jumped out of a window, upsetting three plants. The window was too small for Mr. McGregor, and he was tired of running after Peter. He went back to his work.

Answer the following questions.

1 This question has two parts. First, answer Part A. Then, answer Part B.

Part A

What problem does Peter have in this story?

A. Peter is being chased by Mr. McGregor.

B. Peter has three brothers and sisters.

C. Peter escapes from Mr. McGregor.

D. Mr. McGregor gives up on looking for Peter.

Part B

Which of Peter's actions causes this problem to happen?

A. Peter jumps out a window.

B. Flopsy, Mopsy, and Cotton-tail stay home.

C. Peter hides in a flower pot.

D. Peter doesn't listen to his mother.

> **Hint** What is bothering Peter in this story? Think about what Peter does that leads to this problem.

2 Which of these details from the story **best** shows how Peter Rabbit is different from Flopsy, Mopsy, and Cotton-tail?

A. Peter Rabbit loses his coat and shoes.

B. Peter Rabbit sneezes.

C. Peter Rabbit goes into Mr. McGregor's garden.

D. Peter Rabbit lives in a sand-bank.

> **Hint** What do Peter Rabbit's actions tell you about his character? How is what Peter does different from what the other little rabbits do?

3 Read the sentence from the story, and look at the underlined word.

They lived with their Mother in a sand-bank, <u>underneath</u> the root of a very big fir-tree.

How can you use the word *under* to figure out the meaning of the word <u>underneath</u> in the sentence?

_____

_____

Hint Think about the word you know. Then, reread the whole sentence. How does this word's meaning relate to the rest of the sentence?

4 Read the paragraph about "The Tale of Peter Rabbit" below.

Peter Rabbit's mother says that Peter's father went into Mr. McGregor's garden and ended up being baked into a pie. Peter goes into Mr. McGregor's garden anyway and almost gets caught, too.

Based on this paragraph, which theme **best** fits the story?

A. No garden is safe.

B. Just because something happens once doesn't mean it will happen again.

C. It's fine to steal vegetables when you're hungry.

D. It's important to learn from the mistakes of others.

Hint What happens to Peter because he doesn't listen? What message is the author trying to give by showing these events?

Use the Reading Guide to help you understand the passage.

excerpted and adapted from

The Tale of Benjamin Bunny

by Beatrix Potter

Reading Guide

Which characters in this story have you already met in "The Tale of Peter Rabbit"? Which characters are new in "The Tale of Benjamin Bunny"?

Underline parts of the setting that are the same as the one in "The Tale of Peter Rabbit."

Why is Peter dressed in a handkerchief?

One morning a little rabbit sat on a bank.

He pricked his ears and listened to the trit-trot, trit-trot of a pony.

A gig[1] was coming along the road. It was driven by Mr. McGregor, and beside him sat Mrs. McGregor in her best bonnet.

As soon as they had passed, little Benjamin Bunny slid down into the road, and set off—with a hop, skip, and a jump—to call upon his relations, who lived in the wood at the back of Mr. McGregor's garden.

That wood was full of rabbit holes. And in the neatest, sandiest hole of all lived Benjamin's aunt and his cousins—Flopsy, Mopsy, Cotton-tail, and Peter . . . .

Little Benjamin came round the back of the fir-tree, and nearly tumbled upon the top of his cousin Peter.

Peter was sitting by himself. He looked poorly, and was dressed in a red cotton pocket-handkerchief.

"Peter," said little Benjamin, in a whisper. "Who has got your clothes?"

Peter replied, "The scarecrow in Mr. McGregor's garden," and described how he had been chased about the garden, and had dropped his shoes and coat.

Little Benjamin sat down beside his cousin and assured him that Mr. McGregor had gone out in a gig, and Mrs. McGregor also; and certainly for the day, because she was wearing her best bonnet.

Peter said he hoped that it would rain.

[1] **gig**: a carriage pulled by a horse

At this point old Mrs. Rabbit's voice was heard inside the rabbit hole, calling, "Cotton-tail! Cotton-tail! Fetch some more camomile!"[2]

Peter said he thought he might feel better if he went for a walk.

They went away hand in hand, and got upon the flat top of the wall at the bottom of the wood. From here they looked down into Mr. McGregor's garden. Peter's coat and shoes were plainly to be seen upon the scarecrow, topped with an old tam-o'-shanter of Mr. McGregor's.

Little Benjamin said, "It spoils people's clothes to squeeze under a gate. The proper way to get in is to climb down a pear-tree."

Peter fell down head first. But it was of no consequence, as the bed below was newly raked and quite soft. It had been sown[3] with lettuces.

Little Benjamin said that the first thing to be done was to get back Peter's clothes.

They took them off the scarecrow. There had been rain during the night. There was water in the shoes, and the coat was somewhat shrunk.

Benjamin tried on the tam-o'-shanter, but it was too big for him.

Then he suggested that they should fill the pocket-handkerchief with onions, as a little present for his aunt.

Peter did not seem to be enjoying himself. He kept hearing noises. Benjamin, on the contrary, was perfectly at home, and ate a lettuce leaf. He said that he was in the habit of coming to the garden with his father.

[2] **camomile:** a kind of tea

[3] **sown:** planted

Answer the following question.

1 Read the sentences from "The Tale of Benjamin Bunny" below.

> **Peter's coat and shoes were plainly to be seen upon the scarecrow, topped with an old <u>tam-o'-shanter</u> of Mr. McGregor's . . . .
> Benjamin tried on the tam-o'-shanter, but it was too big for him.**

Based on these sentences, what do you think a <u>tam-o'-shanter</u> is?

A. a type of clothing

B. a type of vegetable

C. a type of rabbit

D. a type of scarecrow

Answer the following questions about both passages in this lesson.

2 Which of these is a true statement about the plots of "The Tale of Peter Rabbit" and "The Tale of Benjamin Bunny"?

A. The plots are exactly the same.

B. The plots are different, but the problem is the same.

C. The plots are different, but the events in the two stories are related.

D. Both plots include a gardener chasing a rabbit.

3 On the lines below, explain how an event from "The Tale of Peter Rabbit" led to the scarecrow wearing Peter's clothes in "The Tale of Benjamin Bunny."

_____

_____

_____

_____

4 Which of the following story parts are the same in "The Tale of Peter Rabbit" and "The Tale of Benjamin Bunny"? Circle **all** that apply.

A. plot

B. setting

C. some of the characters

D. theme

E. point of view

5 The following question has two parts. First, answer Part A. Then, answer Part B.

Part A

Underline a sentence from "The Tale of Benjamin Bunny" that tells how Peter feels while he is in the garden.

Part B

Use what you know about the plot of "The Tale of Peter Rabbit" to explain why Peter feels this way. Then, explain why Benjamin Bunny does not feel this way.

_____

_____

_____

_____

6 "The Tale of Peter Rabbit" and "The Tale of Benjamin Bunny" are from the same collection of short stories. In each story, Peter visits Mr. McGregor's garden. Compare and contrast his experiences in the garden. In your response, be sure to answer the following questions:

- In each story, what is Peter's reason for going to the garden?

- Does he go alone, or is he joined by another character? How does that character help Peter?

- What is the first thing Peter sees in the garden?

- How does each visit end?

Write your answer on the lines below.

_____

_____

_____

_____

_____

_____

_____

_____

_____

_____

_____

_____

_____

_____

Read the passage.

Raven Gives the World Light

Back a long time ago, animals were much like you and me. They talked and lived in houses and did many other things the way we do. At that time, Raven and Seagull lived by the sea in the far North. They were close friends and had houses near each other.

Raven was a clever fellow. He didn't mind lying to other animals or tricking them to get what he wanted. Seagull was quite different. He was as honest as could be and would never try to trick anyone. Perhaps because of his honesty, he never suspected anyone would try to deceive him.

In those days, the world was dark. The only light was from the stars. That was because Seagull owned all the light in the world. He kept it in a box in his house. He only used a little bit from time to time for himself. Light was helpful when he went from place to place.

As you can guess, the other animals wanted light, but Seagull was stingy and wouldn't share. "No. It is mine," he would say. "I want to keep it for myself."

So one day, Raven decided he would trick Seagull into giving him some light. Raven collected thorns and spread them thickly along the path from Seagull's house. Then he returned to Seagull's house and knocked on the door.

"Come quickly," Raven called. "Our canoes are getting caught by the waves. They will get loose and drift away."

Seagull jumped out of bed, where he had been sound asleep. He ran barefoot out the door and down the path. The sharp thorns lodged in his feet, and he screamed in pain. Seagull turned and hobbled back to his house. "Let the canoes float away," he moaned. "My feet are killing me."

Raven muffled a laugh and pretended to pull the canoes up away from the waves. Then he returned to Seagull's house, where Seagull was trying to remove the thorns.

"Here," Raven said. "Let me help. I have done this many times, and I am a very good doctor." Raven picked up a piece of whalebone and began poking at the thorns. Instead of pulling them out, though, he pushed them in more deeply. Seagull howled in pain. "I'm sorry," Raven said. "I can't see in here. It's so dark. Please just let out a little light so I can see what I'm doing."

Seagull had no choice. He unlocked the box containing the light and raised the cover slightly to let just a sliver of light escape.

"That's a little better," Raven said. "I'll try again to get the thorns out."

Once more, Raven set to work, and again he only pushed the thorns deeper.

Seagull yowled loudly and his eyes filled with tears. "You're hurting me!" he screamed.

"Don't complain to me," Raven said. "It's still too dark in here. Why are you so stingy with your light when it's you in such pain?" Then Raven jumped up, pretending to be upset, and in doing so he stumbled against Seagull, who bumped into the box and tipped it over. Light rushed out of the box and spread throughout the world.

Seagull, seeing the light escape, let out the loudest yowl yet. "Look what's happened!" he cried. He tried as hard as he could to collect the light, but it could never be put back into the box.

Raven finished pulling the thorns from Seagull's feet and then walked home. He laughed with glee and looked around at the bright daylight of the world.

Answer the following questions.

1 This question has two parts. First, answer Part A. Then, answer Part B.

Part A

With which statement would the narrator of the story **most likely** agree?

A. Raven is honest and fair.

B. It is unfair of Seagull to keep the light for himself.

C. Raven should be punished for hurting Seagull.

D. The other animals do not deserve to have light.

Part B

Do you agree or disagree with the statement you chose in Part A? Why or why not?

_____

_____

_____

2 This question has two parts. First, answer Part A. Then, answer Part B.

Part A

Read each word in the box. Decide whether the word describes Raven or Seagull. Write the word in the correct column in the chart.

clever	selfish	honest
trusting	crafty	dishonest

Raven	Seagull

Part B

Choose a word that describes Raven. Underline a detail in the passage that shows why the description is true. Circle a word that describes Seagull.

3 Read each sentence from the passage on the left. Draw a line from the sentence to the part of the passage it **best** represents.

A. Raven was a clever fellow. He didn't mind lying to other animals or tricking them to get what he wanted.

B. "Come quickly," Raven called.

C. In those days, the world was dark.

D. So one day, Raven decided he would trick Seagull into giving him some light.

1. setting

2. characters

3. plot event

4. dialogue

4 The following question has two parts. First, answer Part A. Then, answer Part B.

Part A

Read the sentence below. Underline a word that contains a root word and an affix. Circle the affix in the word.

Light was helpful when he went from place to place.

Part B

Write the meaning of the word you chose in Part A on the lines below. Also, write the meaning of the affix it contains.

_____

_____

_____

5 Read these sentences from the passage.

Seagull jumped out of bed, where he had been sound asleep. He ran barefoot out the door and down the path. The sharp thorns lodged in his feet, and he screamed in pain.

Describe what Raven does as a result of this event. How does it lead to the light being released? Include details from the text to support your answer.

_____

_____

_____

_____

_____

_____

_____

Read the passage.

Raven Has a Feast

One summer many, many years ago, Raven played all summer long. It should come as no surprise that Raven enjoyed having a good time and didn't like to work. When Squirrel mentioned that Raven should be putting away food for winter, Raven only laughed. "There's still time for that," he said and flew off to have more fun.

"You'll change your tune when winter arrives," Squirrel called after him. And he was right.

One day, the first flurries of snow drifted from the sky. Soon it was snowing harder, and the earth became covered in its winter blanket. The food that Raven had found so easily all summer was buried.

Feeling hungry, Raven flew over to Squirrel's house. Squirrel had food stashed everywhere. "Squirrel," Raven said, "I'm hungry. Why not share some of your nuts with me?" Squirrel only scolded him. Finally, he shut the door in Raven's face.

Raven flew to the top of a tree and sat thinking. Then he hit upon a plan and flew off to see his cousin Crow.

"Hi, Crow," Raven called out. "I'm looking forward to your feast. Are you going to sing?"

Crow looked puzzled. "I'm not having a feast," he said.

"But you must sing at your feast," Raven said. "You have such a wonderful voice. Everyone wants to hear you."

Crow was flattered by the compliments. In fact, back in those times, Crow did have a nice voice. He started to think maybe he *should* have a feast. "Do you really think I should sing?" he asked.

"Of course," Raven said. "I'll invite everyone to your feast."

Raven visited all the animals. "I'm having a feast," he told each one. "I'm having it at Crow's house, and he will sing for us. Please join me at my feast. I'll have lots of food for everyone."

Then Raven flew back to Crow's home and said, "Prepare all your food, Crow. Everyone is coming, and they are excited to know that you will be singing." Crow got started right away.

On the day of the feast, Raven arrived early and found Crow still cooking. "You finish in the kitchen," Raven said, "and I'll greet the guests as they arrive."

So Raven went to the door. "Welcome to my feast," he said to each guest. "Please eat your fill. It's my great pleasure to have this feast for you."

All the animals sat down at the feast table. When Crow came to join them, Raven spoke up. "Oh please sing for us now, Crow. You cannot sing well on a full stomach." Crow couldn't resist and broke into song. Each time he paused to join the feast, Raven called, "Oh please, one more song. You are in such great voice today." So Crow kept singing, and his voice got tired and hoarse.

When everyone got up from the table to leave, Crow had still not had a bite to eat, and all the food was gone. He was very hungry, and there was no food left in his house. He knew that everyone was grateful, though, and he felt that they would each invite him to a feast. He would not go hungry that winter. But as it turned out, Crow was never invited to any meals. All the animals thought that Raven had given the feast, so they invited him to their meals. Raven did not have to provide for his own winter food for many years.

Poor Crow was left to beg for food from humans and eat the scraps they left. You still see him today hopping about in parks and yards, searching for food and squawking a raspy "Caw! Caw! Caw!"

Answer the following questions.

6 This question has two parts. First, answer Part A. Then, answer Part B.

Part A

Underline an example of nonliteral language in the paragraph below.

> **One day, the first flurries of snow drifted from the sky. Soon it was snowing harder, and the earth became covered in its winter blanket. The food that Raven had found so easily all summer was buried.**

Part B

Choose the **best** meaning of the nonliteral language you underlined in Part A.

A. It snowed lightly at first, and then harder.

B. Raven could not find food.

C. The ground was cold.

D. Snow covered the ground.

7 These events are from the story, but they are out of order. Write the numbers 2, 3, 4, 5, or 6 to put the events in the correct order.

1	Raven did not gather food for winter.
	Crow became hoarse from singing.
	All the animals came to Crow's house for a feast.
	Raven thanked Crow for inviting him to his feast.
	Raven invited the animals to a feast.
	Squirrel refused to give Raven any food.
7	Raven was invited to many feasts.

8 The following question has two parts. First, answer Part A. Then, answer Part B.

Part A

What problem does Raven have in "Raven Has a Feast"?

  A. Raven doesn't know how to cook.

  B. No one will invite Raven to a feast.

  C. Raven doesn't have anything to eat.

  D. Raven cannot sing.

Part B

Which of Raven's actions causes this problem to happen?

  A. Raven lied about having the feast.

  B. Raven refused to share his food.

  C. Raven did not store food for winter.

  D. Raven made his voice hoarse by singing too much.

9 The following question has two parts. First, answer Part A. Then, answer Part B.

Part A

Circle **all** the statements below that correctly describe Raven.

  A. He enjoys playing tricks.

  B. He is thoughtful of others.

  C. He is not always truthful.

  D. He is lazy.

  E. He is practical.

  F. He doesn't have any friends.

Part B

Choose one of the statements you circled in Part A. On the lines, write a detail from either passage that indicates the statement is correct.

_____

_____

_____

_____

PERFORMANCE TASK

"Raven Gives the World Light" and "Raven Has a Feast" are Native American folktales that people told to explain how things in nature came to be. Compare and contrast the central message in each story. What do the messages help the reader understand? In what ways does the character of Raven help reveal each message? Why is he important in both stories? Include details from the text to support your answer.

Write your answer on the lines below.

_____

_____

_____

_____

_____

_____

_____

_____

_____

_____

_____

_____

_____

STRAND 2

Working with Informational Texts

Articles

RI.3.1, RI.3.2; RI.3.4, RI.3.5, RI.3.8, L3.5.b

① GETTING THE IDEA

In fiction writing, the author makes up details to tell a story. In nonfiction writing, the author does not make up details. **Nonfiction** writing gives information about real people, real places, and real things. In fact, some people call it **informational text**. There are many types of nonfiction writing.

Kind of Nonfiction	Purpose
biography	tells the true story of a person's life
speech	tells about a topic through spoken words
textbook	gives facts and details about a topic, such as a social studies or science topic
cookbook	gives directions for how to make different kinds of foods

Another kind of nonfiction is an **article**. You might see articles in newspapers, magazines, and online. An article tells about one topic. All articles are based on facts. A **fact** is a piece of information that can be proved.

Every nonfiction article has a main idea. The **main idea** is the most important thing the author wants you to understand. You can find the main idea by asking, "What is this text mostly about?" Sometimes, an author will tell you the main idea in the title or at the beginning of the text.

Supporting details give more information about the main idea. They help readers understand the main idea, backing it up with evidence such as names, places, dates, and examples.

Read this paragraph about river otters. Circle the main idea. Then, draw a line under the supporting details.

> A river otter is built for the water. Its long body can bend and stretch in the water. Its nostrils and ears close to keep out water when the otter dives. Its webbed feet make it easy for the animal to paddle and swim. Its thick fur keeps the otter warm in cold water. Even the otter's long, flat tail has a job to do. It helps the otter steer.

Text Structure

An author's purpose for writing nonfiction is to inform readers. Authors know they have a lot of information to share. So they are careful to organize the information in a way that makes sense. Authors use different text structures to do this. Text structures include sequence, cause and effect, and compare and contrast.

Sequence In an article that is organized by **sequence**, the facts are in order. It may be in step order with numbers as in a science experiment. It may be in time order and use time-order words, such as *first*, *second*, *next*, *then*, and *last*. Dates and times can also show sequence. Draw a line under the time-order words in this paragraph.

> First, I filled a bird feeder with seeds. Then, I hung the feeder in a tree near our kitchen window. Finally, I sat in the kitchen and looked out the window to watch the birds eat from the feeder.

Cause and Effect Authors use **cause and effect** to explain what happens and why. To find a cause ask, "Why did that happen?" To find an effect ask, "What happens?" The clue words *because*, *cause*, *so*, *therefore*, and *since* can help you find cause-and-effect events. Read this sentence. Draw a line under the cause. Circle the effect.

> The wind blew all night, so the leaves fell from the tree.

Compare and Contrast When authors **compare and contrast**, they tell how things are alike and different. They use words such as *same*, *alike*, *all*, and *different*. Read this paragraph. Underline details that tell how vegetables are alike. Circle details that tell how they are different.

> Vegetables come from different plant parts. Tomatoes come from a plant's seeds. Carrots come from a plant's roots. Lettuce is from a plant's leaves. Vegetables come from different plant parts, but they are all good for you!

Text Features

Authors also use text features to organize ideas. Here are some text features you might see.

- A **heading** tells what a section of text is about. It is shown in bold, or dark, print.

- A **caption** appears under a picture or other visual. It tells what the picture is about.

- **Key words** are words important to a topic. They are often shown in bold print.

- A **sidebar** is a short paragraph next to an article. It gives other interesting facts about a topic.

- A **hyperlink** is a feature in online articles. If you click on a hyperlink, it takes you to another Web page.

Language Spotlight • Real-Life Connections

When you make a connection between a word in your reading and the world, you are identifying a **real-life connection**. Read the example. What real-life connection can you make to help you understand the word *mask*?

> A raccoon is mostly brown with black markings. It has black stripes on its tail and a black <u>mask</u> around its eyes.

Circle the word you could use to replace *mask* in the sentence.

circles   **glasses**   **patches**

Read the passage.

The Giant Panda

The giant panda is a rare and interesting animal. Many people think it is cute and cuddly because of its markings. Like other bears, however, it can be dangerous. Of course, people can be dangerous to pandas, too. That is why there are laws to help protect these animals.

Body Type

A giant panda has black fur on its legs, shoulders, and ears, and around its eyes and mouth. The rest of the body is covered in white fur. The panda's thick fur keeps it warm in the cool mountain forests.

An adult panda can weigh up to 250 pounds. Standing on all four legs, it is between two and three feet tall. From its nose to tail, it measures four to six feet long.

The giant panda has a long wrist bone in each front paw. This bone acts like a thumb. It helps the panda hold its food while it eats. The panda also has a strong jaw and big teeth. The teeth are wide and flat. This helps the animal eat bamboo, its favorite food. Bamboo is a tall plant with a stiff stem.

Diet

In the wild, about 99 percent of a giant panda's diet is bamboo. The other one percent is grasses, bugs, fish, and small animals. Bamboo is not very <u>nutritious</u>. To stay healthy, a giant panda has to eat twenty to forty pounds of bamboo a day. A panda spends about half of each day gathering and eating bamboo.

This giant panda is using its front paws to eat bamboo.

Habitat

In the wild, giant pandas live in bamboo forests high in the mountains. The mountains are located in a small area of China. Pandas move from mountain to mountain to find the bamboo that grows on the mountaintops.

Saving Pandas

People now use much of the land on which the pandas once lived. People live and work in the valleys between the mountains. This stops the pandas from moving from one mountain to another to find the bamboo that grows there. Many pandas cannot find the food they need. Now the giant panda is an endangered animal. There are only about 1,600 pandas left in the wild.

China is trying to save the pandas. One idea is to keep strips of land between the mountains clear of people. Chinese government workers plant bamboo on the strips of land. The pandas can follow the strips to the next mountain.

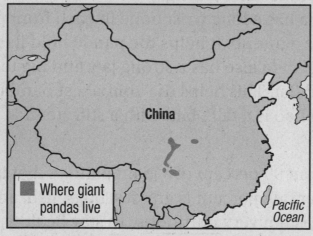

The shaded area on the map shows where giant pandas live in the wild.

Answer the following questions.

1 What is the article **mostly** about?

A. China

B. giant pandas

C. bamboo

D. mountains

Hint Look at the title and the headings. What do they all tell about?

2 Read the sentences from the article and the questions that follow.

Bamboo is not very <u>nutritious</u>. To stay healthy, a giant panda has to eat twenty to forty pounds of bamboo a day.

Part A

What does the word <u>nutritious</u> mean?

A. healthy

B. unhealthy

C. stems

D. pounds

Part B

What do you eat that is nutritious? Why do you think it is nutritious?

Write your answer on the lines below.

_____

_____

_____

_____

Hint For Part A, think about how the article uses the word *nutritious* and how you use it to make a real-life connection. Then, show your understanding of the word to answer Part B.

3 Under which heading in the article would you look to learn about what the Chinese government is doing to help giant pandas?

   A. Body Type

   B. Diet

   C. Habitat

   D. Saving Pandas

> **Hint** Remember that a heading tells what a section of a text is about. Which heading tells about helping pandas?

4 The following question has two parts. First, answer Part A. Then, answer Part B.

Part A

How are the sentences under the heading "Saving Pandas" organized?

   A. sequence

   B. step order

   C. cause and effect

   D. compare and contrast

Part B

Why is it difficult for pandas to find the food they need? Choose **all** that apply.

   A. People now use much of the land on which the pandas once lived on.

   B. People live and work in the valleys between the mountains.

   C. Now the giant panda is an endangered animal.

   D. There are only about 1,600 pandas left in the wild.

> **Hint** Look back at the section "Saving Pandas" to answer Part A. Are the sentences organized in order, or do they tell what happens and why? For Part B, look for the causes that explain why the pandas have trouble finding food.

Use the Reading Guide to help you understand the passage.

Too Cute!

Reading Guide

Why does the author talk about certain parts of the face in paragraphs 3 and 4?

Find the word *same* in paragraph 4. What does that clue word tell the reader?

How does the author answer the question in the heading?

People gather around a puppy in the park. When they visit a zoo, the first thing they want to see is the new baby elephant or panda. Or, they crowd around to see a baby monkey riding on its mother's back. What is it about these animals that draws a crowd? Experts say it can be explained through science.

What Makes Something Cute?

Scientists think our idea of what makes something cute is planted in our brains. Because human babies cannot survive without help, our brain makes us see babies as cute so we will want to take care of them.

What does this have to do with animals? Think about a human baby. Babies have round heads that seem large for their bodies. They have big eyes and small noses. They have chubby cheeks and round ears. Their round bodies and loose skin make them look soft. The human brain identifies these features as cute.

Now picture a baby animal, such as a puppy or a kitten. Do the same <u>features</u> come to mind? Most baby animals also have big eyes, small noses or snouts, round ears, and big cheeks. Scientists believe that because our brain likes these features in human babies, we like animal babies for the same reasons.

A baby harp seal has a rounded body and big eyes, just like a human baby.

Why does the author give examples of animal actions, such as a giraffe taking its first steps or a monkey clinging to its mother?

How do zoos use the appeal of baby animals to bring in visitors?

How Do Cute Babies Act?

Scientists think it is more than a cute face that makes people love baby animals. They think it is also how baby animals act. People like to watch actions that remind them of how human babies move. Think about a human baby's first wobbly steps. Then, picture a baby penguin or giraffe taking its first steps. The unsure side-to-side motion is much like that of a human baby.

Now think about other things that make people "ooh" and "aah" at the zoo. It may be tiger cubs rolling around on the ground. It may be a monkey clinging to its mother or a young panda curling up for a nap. Actions that are clumsy, playful, or loving all remind us of human babies.

How Does Cuteness Help Zoos?

When a new baby is born or adopted at a zoo, the zoo workers are happy. They know that people will come to see the new baby animal. Some zoos hold contests in which the winners get to name the new baby. Sometimes, zoos offer special programs so visitors can meet new babies and learn about them. These events bring lots of people to the zoo or aquarium.

So the next time you rush to see a puppy or kitten, look carefully. Does it remind you of a human baby? If it does, your brain is telling you that the animal is cute.

A mother giraffe helps her baby take its first steps.

Answer the following questions.

1 Read these sentences from the article and the directions that follow.

Now picture a baby animal, such as a puppy or a kitten. Do the same <u>features</u> come to mind? Most baby animals also have big eyes, small noses or snouts, round ears, and big cheeks.

What does the word <u>features</u> mean in the sentence?

A. things that all look alike

B. interesting or important parts

C. special stories in a newspaper or magazine

D. pays special attention to

2 Which sentence supports the main idea in the section "How Do Cute Babies Act?" Choose **all** that apply.

A. A baby harp seal has a rounded body and big eyes, just like a human baby.

B. Scientists think it is more than a cute face that makes people love animals.

C. People like to watch actions that remind them of how human babies move.

D. Actions that are clumsy, playful, or loving all remind us of human babies.

E. So the next time you rush to see a puppy or kitten, look carefully.

3 What does the author say about how cute baby animals help zoos?

A. Zoos put pictures of the animals in magazines and online.

B. Zoos let visitors adopt the new animal babies.

C. Zoos hold contests to name the animals and offer special programs.

D. Zoos sometimes have new or adopted baby animals.

4 According to the article, what makes a baby animal look cute?

Write your answer on the lines below.

_____

_____

_____

5 The following question has two parts. First, answer Part A. Then, answer part B.

Part A

Which **two** text features are used in the article?

A. sidebars

B. captions

C. hyperlinks

D. headings

Part B

How do the photographs help you understand the main idea of the article?

A. The photographs show cute animal babies and their mothers.

B. The photographs show unusual animals in the wild.

C. The photographs show how some cute animals look and act.

D. The photographs show adult animals.

6 Tell about the article "Too Cute!" in your own words. Identify the main idea and the details that support it.

Use evidence from the text to support your answer.

Write your answer on the lines below.

_____

_____

_____

_____

_____

_____

_____

_____

_____

_____

_____

_____

_____

_____

_____

_____

_____

_____

RI.3.1, RI.3.2, RI.3.4, RI.3.6, RI.3.8, L.3.6

Persuasive Texts

A **persuasive text** is used to persuade, or convince, people. Authors write persuasive texts for different reasons. They may want readers to agree with an idea. Or, they may want readers to take a specific action.

Persuasive writing is all around you. Advertisements in newspapers and magazines are persuasive texts. They encourage you to buy certain products. Or they persuade you to do things, like recycle. Many newspapers and magazines also have an editorial section. In this section, editors write persuasive texts to give their opinions about issues in the community. Readers may choose to write back to the editor. They write to give their opinions about news stories or opinions stated in articles.

Structure

In a persuasive text, an author:

- gives a main opinion on a topic.
- offers reasons why readers should believe the opinion.
- gives facts to back up the opinion.
- asks the reader for an action or a response.
- provides a concluding statement or section to sum up the information.

Authors may organize the information in a persuasive text in different ways.

Problem and Solution Some persuasive texts use a problem-and-solution structure. The author gives facts about a **problem** and an opinion about a **solution**, or how the problem can be solved. To back up the opinion, the author gives reasons why the solution is a good idea.

Main Idea and Supporting Details Most persuasive texts use a **main idea** and details structure. Usually the author states the main idea at the beginning of the text. Then, the rest of the text includes **supporting details** about the main idea.

The main idea in a persuasive text is often based on the author's opinion. **Opinions** are statements that are based on personal feelings. They cannot be proven true. The author provides reasons and facts that back up his or her opinion. **Facts** are pieces of information that are true and can be proven. Read the sentences below.

> **Opinion:** Board games are fun.
> **Fact:** Some board games are played in teams.

Notice the difference between a fact and an opinion. The opinion is a personal belief. It cannot be proven true. Other people may have the opposite opinion. They may think that board games are not fun. The fact, however, is a true statement. It can be proven that some board games are played in teams.

Read this paragraph. Circle the author's main opinion.

> Children should play more board games. Board games can help children learn vocabulary words, math concepts, and other facts. Many board games ask players to use words. This can help children practice their spelling skills. Children can also learn new words. Some games use play money. These games can help children practice adding and subtracting numbers. Other games ask questions about trivia facts. Children can learn more about topics like science and history.

In this paragraph, the author believes that children should play more board games. The author supports this main opinion with reasons and facts. The reasons tell how board games can help children learn. The facts tell about the specific features of some games.

Methods of Persuasion

Writers use different ways to persuade you to agree with their opinions. A writer may say that everyone likes a particular activity or product, so you should, too. For example, "Most parents know that board games help kids learn." Writers also use strong words that affect a reader's emotions. A writer may use words such as *harmful*, *suffer*, *important*, and *necessary*.

Point of View

A persuasive text is built around a point of view. The **point of view** is the author's opinion about an issue. Authors give facts that support their opinions. Often, authors mention opposite views, but then they show why those views are wrong.

You may not always agree with the author's point of view in a persuasive text. But this does not mean that the text is not well written. It also does not mean that the author did not support his or her opinion well.

Think about the author's opinion and the reasons and facts presented. If you can answer *yes* to these questions, then the text is likely a well-written persuasive text.

- Is the author convincing?

- Does the author give enough reasons to show why people should agree with his or her opinion?

- Does the author use facts to back up his or her opinion?

Language Spotlight • Academic Vocabulary

Academic vocabulary includes words that apply to general subjects. The words *facts* and *opinion* are both academic words. Use each word twice to complete the sentences below.

Read this history article with _____ about life in colonial times. Then, give your _____ about what life was like back then. Write a persuasive text to give an _____. Use _____ to support your ideas.

Read the passage.

Video Games Are Good for Kids

People may question whether video games make children lazy. They may wonder if children waste too much time playing them. But there are many video games available today. Many are educational. Some involve physical motion. Others support teamwork and cooperation. Video games can be good for children. We should encourage children to play them.

First, educational games can help children learn. Children can use these games to learn new words. Some games can help children practice math skills. Video games can help make learning more fun. Children are more likely to learn and hold onto information when they are having fun.

Video games can also help kids with problem solving. In some games, players work through problems. Usually a player has to complete a task before he or she can move on to the next level. Kids have to reason and think about what they are doing. If they choose incorrectly, they can redo a portion of the game and try another method. This helps them solve problems.

Other video games help kids get exercise. This may seem like a strange idea, but new technology has changed the way some video games are played. Some gaming systems use a special camera that can track movement. Children can be active while playing these games. They may run in place, jump, or dance to play a game. Their movements are shown on the screen and help them earn points. Many of these games also have children play together and work as a team. They can learn cooperation and other social skills while playing.

So, don't be afraid to let your kids play video games. If anything, you should tell them to play more. Playing can help them learn, improve their social skills, and be physically active. Knowing all of those benefits, why would anyone discourage video game play?

Answer the following questions.

1 This question has two parts. First, answer Part A. Then, answer Part B.

Part A

What is the author trying persuade the reader to do?

A. buy a video game

B. agree that video games are good for kids

C. give video games to schools

D. create new educational video games

Part B

Which statement from the passage **best** supports your answer to Part A?

A. People may question whether video games make children lazy.

B. Children are more likely to learn and hold onto information when they are having fun.

C. This may seem like a strange idea, but new technology has changed the way some video games are played.

D. So, don't be afraid to let your kids play video games.

Hint Think about the main idea in the passage. Which of these answer choices fits with the main idea? Your answer to Part B should support your answer to Part A.

2 Which statement from the passage is a fact?

A. Video games can help make learning more fun.

B. They may run in place, jump, or dance to play a game.

C. This helps them solve problems.

D. If anything, you should tell them to play more.

Hint Remember that a fact is a true statement that can be proven.

3 Read the sentence from the passage and the question that follows.

> **If they choose incorrectly, they can redo a portion of the game and try another method.**

How does this sentence relate to the reason that video games can help kids with problem solving?

A. It gives an example of how children can practice problem solving.

B. It tells why video games make it harder for children to problem solve.

C. It explains the history of how video games have helped kids problem solve.

D. It compares video game learning to video game problem solving.

> **Hint** Reread paragraph 3 in the passage. How does the information in the sentence relate to the rest of the paragraph?

4 The author ends the passage by stating: "Knowing all of those benefits, why would anyone discourage video game play?" Why does the author make this statement? What effect might it have on the reader?

Write your answer on the lines below.

_____

_____

_____

_____

> **Hint** Remember why authors use a conclusion in a persuasive text. What view does the author want the reader to agree with?

Use the Reading Guide to help you understand the passage.

The Dangers of Video Games

Reading Guide

How does the title of the passage help you understand the author's point of view?

What is the author's main opinion about video games?

What facts does the author give to back up his or her opinion?

Why do parents allow their children to play so many video games? Kids already spend too much time in front of screens. They watch TV, surf the Internet, and use tablets. Add in video games, and problems increase even more. Video games keep kids from spending time with friends and family. Too often, video games replace outdoor fun. Schoolwork suffers. Parents have to remind their kids to do chores. Because of all these problems, parents should limit or ban video games for their kids.

Children already have too much screen time. Screen time is any time kids spend in front of a computer or other device that has a screen. According to one study, many children spend five to seven hours in front of a screen each day. Too much screen time can affect children's health and well-being. They may gain weight. They may also have a hard time paying attention or falling asleep at night.

Playing video games is an inactive hobby. And too much inactivity is not good for kids' health. Kids will sit and play for long periods of time. Too much time sitting means not enough exercise. To live an active, healthy life, kids need to move. Researchers at an organization called KidsHealth found that kids who exercise more have a better outlook on life.

Kids who play video games less often may also develop better relationship skills. When children play too many video games, relationships with friends and family suffer. Quality time is limited.

How does the author use strong language to affect the reader?

How does the conclusion sum up the topic?

Is the author convincing? Why or why not?

Even when kids play video games with friends, they often focus on the game instead of talking. This isn't true for other types of games. For example, kids may play a group sport such as kickball or baseball. They talk to each other. They work together as a team. Children can build better friendships when they turn the video games off.

Finally, video games can be harmful to children's schoolwork. Some kids spend more time playing than working on homework. People have done studies that show that kids who play video games spend 34 percent less time doing homework. Other studies show that more than one or two hours a day of screen time can lead to lower test scores. This may be because video games can affect children's ability to pay attention. So, grades and overall learning suffer. Sure, some video games can be educational. But kids enjoy the silly or most popular games more. How often do they really play learning games?

Overall, video games are not a good choice for kids. Children need fresh air, exercise, and time away from screens. They need to spend more face-to-face time with others. Most of all, they need to focus on homework and doing well in school. So unless you want your kids to suffer in all areas of their lives, you should keep them away from video games!

Answer the following questions.

1 This question has two parts. First, answer Part A. Then, answer Part B.

Part A

What is the author's point of view about video games?

A. Video games can sometimes be educational.

B. Video games are too expensive for most families.

C. Video games can be played in groups.

D. Video games are not good for kids.

Part B

Write one sentence from the passage to support your answer to Part A.

_____

_____

_____

2 Which statement **best** explains what the author wants readers to do?

A. They should find new kinds of video games for their children.

B. They should limit children's time playing video games.

C. They should tell children to exercise more.

D. They should encourage children to do more chores at home.

3 Write the sentences from the box in the correct locations on the chart. Show how the author introduces the main opinion and provides details to support it.

Sentences	Kids who play video games spend 34 percent less time doing homework.
	Parents should limit or ban video game time for kids.
	Video games can be harmful to children's schoolwork.

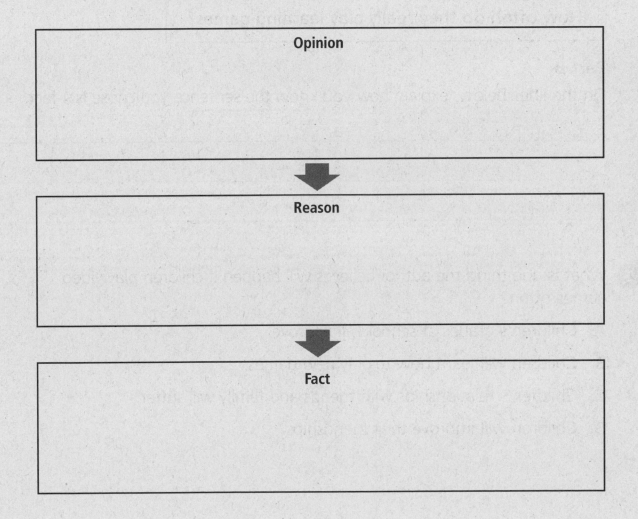

Opinion

Reason

Fact

4 The following question has two parts. First, answer Part A. Then, answer Part B.

Part A

Below are three statements from the passage. Circle the sentence that is a fact.

Children already have too much screen time.
According to one study, many children spend five to seven hours in front of a screen each day.
How often do they really play learning games?

Part B

On the lines below, explain how you know the sentence you chose is a fact.

_____

_____

_____

5 What is one thing the author believes will happen if children play video games often?

A. Children's grades at school will improve.

B. Children will learn how to play new games.

C. Children's relationships with friends and family will suffer.

D. Children will improve their friendships.

6 The authors of "Video Games Are Good for Kids" and "The Dangers of Video Games" have different opinions about video games. Which one do you agree with? Do you think video games are helpful or harmful to children? How does the information in each passage relate to your own point of view?

Use details from each text to explain your answer.

Write your answer on the lines below.

_____

_____

_____

_____

_____

_____

_____

_____

_____

_____

_____

_____

_____

_____

_____

RI.3.1, RI.3.2, RI.3.3, RI.3.4, RI.3.7, RI.3.8, L.3.6

Historical Texts

1 GETTING THE IDEA

A **historical text** tells about real events, real people, or real places from long ago. Historical texts can tell:

- how people lived.
- when and where events took place.
- where places were and what they looked like.
- how the past and the present connect.

The purpose of a historical text may be to inform or persuade readers. When the purpose is to inform, most authors present the facts and details without sharing their point of view. When the purpose is to persuade, authors try to encourage readers to think a certain way or to do something.

Types of Historical Texts

Different types of historical texts give different information. Read the chart below.

Historical Text	Definition
speech	a spoken opinion or report about a topic
document	an official paper about a law or an agreement
nonfiction book	a text that gives facts and details about a topic from history
biography	a book that tells the true story of a person's life

Main Idea and Details

Like other nonfiction texts, the **main idea** of a historical text is what the text is mostly about. **Supporting details** give important information about the main idea. They help readers understand the main idea by backing it up with evidence.

Read this paragraph. Circle the main idea and underline the supporting details.

> Neil Armstrong's love of flight began with an airplane ride when he was six. From then on, he wanted to fly higher and faster. He flew model airplanes and learned to fly a real plane before he could drive a car. As an adult, Armstrong was a Navy pilot, an airplane designer, and an astronaut. He flew his highest and fastest on a trip to the moon. On July 20, 1968, Neil Armstrong became the first person to walk on the moon.

Text Structure

Text structure is how a text is organized. The most common structures in historical texts are cause-and-effect and sequence.

A **cause-and-effect** structure explains why different things happen. It shows how events are connected. A **cause** is the event that happens first. The **effect** is what happens as a result of the cause. Authors use signal words to show cause and effect. These include *because*, *for this reason*, *due to*, and *as a result*.

Read these sentences. Underline the cause and circle the effect. Draw a box around cause-and-effect signal words.

> The Declaration of Independence was signed on July 4, 1776. As a result, we celebrate Independence Day every year on the fourth of July.

A **sequence** structure tells events in order. Dates and time-order words help identify the sequence of events. Time-order words include *first, then, before, after,* and *finally*.

Circle the words that show sequence in this paragraph.

> On January 24, 1848, gold was discovered in California. At first, the discovery was a secret. Then, a newspaper printed a story about the gold. Soon many people were traveling to California to look for gold. By the end of 1849, the number of settlers living in California had grown from 1,000 to 100,000.

Graphic Features

Graphic features, such as diagrams and maps, are visual aids that help explain the text or give extra information. Here are some examples of graphic features in historical texts.

- A **map** is a drawing that shows where places or things are located.

- A **timeline** shows when events happened. The dates and events are shown in time order along a line or bar.

Oregon Trail Events

First wagon train leaves from Independence, Missouri, carrying 47 people.

Nearly 5,000 travelers leave from Independence and Westport, Missouri.

Nearly 1,000 people leave from Elm Grove, Missouri.

Mormon settlers leave Illinois and settle in Utah.

- A **photograph** is a picture that shows an event as it really happened. This photograph shows President Theodore Roosevelt making a speech many years ago.

- An **illustration** is a drawing that shows what something looks like. A **caption** gives more information about it.

Covered wagon pulled by oxen

Language Spotlight • Domain-Specific Vocabulary

In historical texts, you may see **domain-specific vocabulary,** or words that relate to a certain topic. These words may be unfamiliar because they are not used in everyday language. Context clues, a glossary, or a dictionary can help you learn what the words mean. Read the paragraph. Circle the words that name Native American homes.

Native Americans built many different kinds of homes. Some lived in dome-shaped wigwams covered with sheets of tree bark. Several Iroquois families could live in one longhouse, which looked like a long, wide wigwam. The Plains Indians lived in tentlike structures called tepees.

Read the passage.

Wagons West

In the 1830s and 1840s, most Americans lived on the East Coast. It was the only settled part of our country. As a result, the area was crowded. Land was hard to find.

Many traders, though, had been out west. They returned with exciting stories. The Oregon Territory had plenty of open land. It had great soil for crops. This news excited many people. Some Americans wanted a new opportunity. Adventurers wanted excitement. So, thousands of families decided to move west. They packed up their belongings and traveled along the Oregon Trail, a two thousand-mile route between Missouri and the Oregon Valley.

The <u>pioneers</u> began their trip in early spring. These first settlers wanted to reach Oregon before winter. But they had to wait for grass to grow. The animals needed the grass to eat along the trail. Most people left from Independence, Missouri. Others joined from smaller towns along the way.

The trip was difficult. The only way to go was by wagon train, which was a group of wagons pulled by horses, mules, or oxen. Each wagon could hold about five people. A trip could last five months.

Moving west was a big decision because it cost so much money. Families spent around $1,000 for their food supply and wagon. This was a huge amount of money for families long ago, when people usually earned only a few dollars each week.

Families took as many supplies and household goods as their animals could pull. But the wagons could hold only so much. Therefore, many people had to sell or leave some things behind. Selling some of what they had, though, helped to pay for the trip.

Getting ready was key. There was not much to buy or trade along the route. So, supplies for the entire trip had to be carried in the wagon train. Travelers had to bring all of their food, such as flour, coffee, and salt. They brought all their tools for cooking and eating. They packed all of their bedding, towels, clothing, and shoes. They packed seeds and farming tools to grow crops. They brought weapons for protection and hunting.

Whatever the reason people made the trip west, it took planning and courage. Following the Oregon Trail was hard. The pioneers who braved it changed both their own lives and America.

Answer the following questions.

1 Match each cause on the left with its effect on the right.

A. Only the East Coast was settled.	**1.** People packed up and moved west.
B. Families wanted more land or opportunity.	**2.** Families had to sell some of their belongings.
C. All supplies had to fit in the wagons.	**3.** Cities and towns were overcrowded.

> **Hint** Remember that a cause is an event that makes another event happen.

2 Read both parts of the question before responding.

Part A

What is a main idea of "Wagons West"?

A. Most Americans in the mid-1800s lived on the East Coast.

B. Families had to prepare for their journey on the Oregon Trail.

C. Horses, mules, and oxen were used to pull wagons.

D. Pioneers had a hard time settling a new area.

Part B

Which details from the text support the main idea in Part A? Circle **all** that apply.

A. Each wagon could hold about five people.

B. Travelers had to bring all of their food, such as flour, coffee, and salt.

C. . . . people usually earned only a few dollars each week.

D. They packed all of their bedding, towels, clothing, and shoes.

E. They packed seeds and farming tools to grow crops.

> **Hint** Think about an important idea in the text. Then, look for facts that tell about that idea.

3 Read the paragraph from the passage and the directions that follow.

> **The <u>pioneers</u> began their trip in early spring. These first settlers wanted to reach Oregon before winter. But they had to wait for grass to grow. The animals needed the grass to eat along the trail. Most people left from Independence, Missouri. Others joined from smaller towns along the way.**

Underline the words in the paragraph that explain the meaning of the word <u>pioneers</u>.

Hint Look for clues around *pioneers* to help you figure out its meaning.

4 The following question has two parts. First, answer Part A. Then, answer Part B.

Part A

Where did the Oregon Trail end?

A. Fort Kearny, Nebraska

B. Fort Laramie, Wyoming

C. Independence, Missouri

D. Oregon City, Oregon

Part B

How did you find the answer to Part A?

Write your answer on the lines below.

_____

_____

_____

Hint Reread paragraphs 2 and 3 of the passage. Then study the map. What can you conclude about the end of the trail?

Use the Reading Guide to help you understand the passage.

Children on the Oregon Trail

In 1851, Martha Gay Masterson left her home in Springfield, Missouri. She was sad and scared to leave. At the age of thirteen, she faced a long journey. Her family was starting on the Oregon Trail.

Like Martha, most children who made the trip west were sad. Their move was <u>permanent</u>. They would probably never again see the friends and family they left behind.

What was it like for children on the Oregon Trail? It was a trip of both challenges and thrills. Storms and high winds blew across the land. Children slept on the ground, sometimes without a tent. They were often hungry and tired. Because their wagon was full, they walked most of the trip. That meant that even young children would walk about fifteen miles each day.

Children also had many chores to do. The long day started around 4:00 a.m. If the family had cows, children would herd and milk them. Then, they would gather wood or fetch water. If there was no wood, children collected buffalo chips to burn instead. Buffalo chips are dried buffalo waste. After children did their own chores, they helped their mothers cook and wash.

Which details tell that the trip was dangerous?

Which details tell about the pleasant parts of the trip?

Why were children ready to start their lives in Oregon? Identify the cause and effect in the last paragraph.

Life on the trail could be more than hard. It could be dangerous. Many people did not survive. Disease and accidents were the biggest risks. They claimed the lives of both children and adults. Brothers, sisters, and mothers sometimes drowned while crossing rivers. Children could fall under the wheels of a moving wagon.

The journey west was not all suffering, though. There were adventures, too. Pioneers crossed miles of beautiful, open grasslands. Millions of grazing buffalo covered the land. Children explored hot springs, waterfalls, and other natural features. They picked wildflowers, danced around campfires, and met Native Americans.

Children on the Oregon Trail were probably happy that there was no school. They did have time, though, for learning. Families had brought books along, so children could read nearly every day. Younger children were taught to read. Mothers helped their children with math and history. Many children wrote about their adventures in journals.

Children found ways to have fun. They created new games using buffalo chips. Telling rhymes, riddles, or jokes helped pass the time. Music did, too. Families sang hymns, ballads, and rounds. They played musical instruments such as fiddles and flutes that they had packed in the wagons.

When children reached the end of the Oregon Trail, they were about five months older. They were dirty and tired. The hard trip forced them to grow up fast. Now they were ready to start their new lives in the Oregon Territory.

Answer the following questions.

1 This question has two parts. First, answer Part A. Then, answer Part B.

Part A

Read this paragraph from "Children on the Oregon Trail" and the directions that follow.

> **Children also had many chores to do. The long day started around 4:00 a.m. If the family had cows, children would herd and milk them. Then, they would gather wood or fetch water. If there was no wood, children collected buffalo chips to burn instead. Buffalo chips are dried buffalo waste. After children did their own chores, they helped their mothers cook and wash.**

What text structure organizes the paragraph? Write your answer on the line below.

_____

Part B

Circle three examples of signal words that helped you identify the structure of the paragraph.

2 Read these sentences from the text.

Life on the trail could be more than hard. It could be dangerous. Many people did not survive. Disease and accidents were the biggest risks. They claimed the lives of both children and adults.

Which statement describes how the sentences are organized?

A. The sentences describe a sequence of events.

B. The sentences tell how two events are different.

C. The sentences describe a problem and a solution.

D. The sentences explain a cause and effect.

3 Read both parts of the question before responding.

Part A

Which sentence **best** tells the main idea of "Children on the Oregon Trail"?

A. Her family was starting on the Oregon Trail.

B. Like Martha, most children who made the trip west were sad.

C. It was a trip of both challenges and thrills.

D. That meant that even young children would walk about fifteen miles each day.

Part B

Which sentences from the text support your answer to Part A? Circle **all** that apply.

A. What was it like for children on the Oregon Trail?

B. Children slept on the ground, sometimes without a tent.

C. They picked wildflowers, danced around campfires, and met Native Americans.

D. In 1851, Martha Gay Masterson left her home in Springfield, Missouri.

4 Read this paragraph from the passage and the directions that follow.

> **Like Martha, most children who made the trip west were sad. Their move was <u>permanent</u>. They would probably never again see the friends and family they left behind.**

What phrase or sentence from the paragraph explains the meaning of the word <u>permanent</u>? Write your answer on the lines below. Then, write the meaning of the word <u>permanent</u>.

_____

_____

_____

_____

5 How were children who traveled on the Oregon Trail able to continue learning, even though they did not go to school?

Write your answer on the lines below.

_____

_____

_____

_____

6 What was daily life like for children traveling on the Oregon Trail? Use specific details from **both** the illustration and the text to support your answer.

Write your answer on the lines below.

_____

_____

_____

_____

_____

_____

_____

_____

_____

_____

_____

_____

_____

_____

RI.3.1, RI.3.2, RI.3.3, RI.3.4, RI.3.7, RI.3.8, L.3.6

Scientific and Technical Texts

❶ GETTING THE IDEA

Two kinds of nonfiction texts are scientific texts and technical texts. A **scientific text** informs readers about a science topic, such as how plants grow. A science textbook and an experiment are two examples of scientific texts. A **technical text** gives details about how something works or instructions on how to do something. Instructions for hooking up a video game console and a cookbook recipe are two examples.

Main Idea and Details

All scientific and technical texts have a **main idea** that tells what the text is mostly about. They also have **supporting details** that explain and back up the main idea. When the main idea tells how to do something, as in an experiment or a recipe, the details are the steps you follow. When the main idea shares the results of an experiment, the details explain what happened.

Read this sample text. Underline the main idea. What are the supporting details?

My experiment showed that dark materials absorb, or take in, more heat than light ones. To begin, I got two thermometers, a black cloth, and a white cloth. Each thermometer measured 67°F at the start of the experiment. Next, I wrapped one thermometer in the black cloth and one in the white cloth. Then, I placed both cloths in the sunlight. After one hour, I checked the thermometers. The thermometer in the black cloth read 81°F. The one in the white cloth read 77°F. My experiment proved that dark materials absorb more heat than light ones.

Text Structure

Text structure is how a text is organized. Here are some common ways authors organize scientific and technical texts.

Steps in a Process Texts that explain how to do something show the **steps in a process**. Each step must be done in order or the process won't work as planned. Numbers, bullets, and time-order words can show the order of steps. Look back at the experiment with the thermometers. How does the author show steps in a process?

Part to Whole A **part-to-whole** text structure starts with the main idea, or the "whole." The supporting details are the "parts." What is the "whole" in the paragraph below? What are the "parts"?

> A bicycle is a simple machine. The body of a bicycle is the frame. Attached to the frame are a seat, handlebars, wheels, and pedals. To make a bicycle move, riders push down on the pedals. The pedals turn a chain connected to the rear wheel.

Problem and Solution In texts organized by **problem and solution**, authors state a problem and suggest ways to solve it. Circle the problem in the paragraph below. Underline the solution.

> Hiccups can be a problem. One solution is to breathe into a paper bag. Hold the end of the paper bag around your mouth as you breathe.

Cause and Effect When authors use **cause and effect**, they explain what happens and why. The words *because*, *since*, and *as a result* can signal cause and effect. Underline the cause and circle the effect below.

> Heavy rains caused the river to rise and overflow. As a result, the streets flooded.

Spatial The word *spatial* means "relating to space." A **spatial** text structure organizes details by the space they take up. A text about layers of soil may use the signal words *top*, *middle*, and *bottom* to describe the different layers. Other spatial words include *north*, *south*, *left,* and *right*.

Graphic Features

Scientific and technical texts often include graphic features. A **graphic feature** is a visual aid that helps readers understand information. Here are some kinds of graphic features found in scientific and technical texts.

A **diagram** is a drawing that shows the parts of something or how something works. In the example below, labels name some parts of an insect.

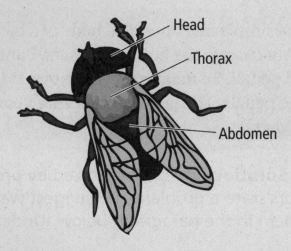

A **flowchart** is a chart that shows the steps in a process. The flowchart below tells how some mud wasps build their nests.

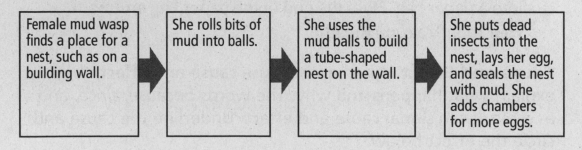

Female mud wasp finds a place for a nest, such as on a building wall. → She rolls bits of mud into balls. → She uses the mud balls to build a tube-shaped nest on the wall. → She puts dead insects into the nest, lays her egg, and seals the nest with mud. She adds chambers for more eggs.

The **table** on the left shows information in columns and rows. A **graph** shows information in a visual way. The bar graph on the right shows the same facts as the table. How does the graph make it easy to see the different plant heights?

Plant Height in Inches	
Plant	**Inches**
Plant 1	4
Plant 2	2.5
Plant 3	3.5
Plant 4	4

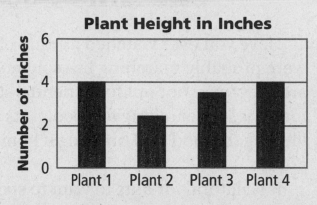

Plant Height in Inches

Language Spotlight • Domain-Specific Vocabulary

Like historical texts, scientific and technical texts can have **domain-specific vocabulary,** or words that relate to a topic. Even if you recognize a word, its meaning may be different when it is used with a particular topic. Use context clues, a glossary, or a dictionary to help you determine the meaning of domain-specific words.

Read the paragraph. Underline domain-specific words that name and tell about Earth's layers. Use context clues or a dictionary to figure out what the words mean.

Earth is made up of different layers. The surface is the crust. It is made of rock. Beneath the crust is the mantle. The mantle contains hot, melted rock. Next comes the outer core. It is made up of melted iron and nickel. The inner core is the center of Earth. It is solid iron and nickel.

Read the passage.

The Ants Go Marching

Have you ever watched a group of ants out for a walk? They were probably marching like soldiers, in a single line. Chances are they were not out for a friendly stroll. They were most likely foraging, or searching for food. Ants spend most of their time looking for food and bringing it home. They do this work in groups.

It is natural for ants to want to stay together. Thousands of ants live together in a large group called a colony. The colony works together to build an anthill with a nest inside. Many different trails and tunnels lead to and from the nest. Some tunnels go deep into the ground and lead to water. Others lead to food sources.

With thousands of ants and so many trails, life could get complicated. But the ants always know where they are going. How do they stay on the right path? What keeps them from getting lost? The answer is both simple and amazing. Ants give off scents called <u>pheromones</u> that other ants follow. These signals act like road signs that guide the colony. As a result, the ants do not get lost. Pheromones are chemicals that only other ants can smell. Ants do not have noses like people do, so they pick up the scents with the antennae on their heads.

Ants are always looking for food. Scouts head out first and leave a pheromone trail as they move toward the food sources they find. Then, other ants follow the trails to the food and bring it back to the nest. Because strong pheromone smells attract ants, they will follow them. If the smell is weak, they look for another route. Scents fade over time. That keeps ants from following an old path that does not lead to food.

You might not like it if ants get into your house or picnic basket, but they are remarkable creatures. The next time you see them marching in a line or twitching their antennae, think about how they are picking up pheromones and working together to find food!

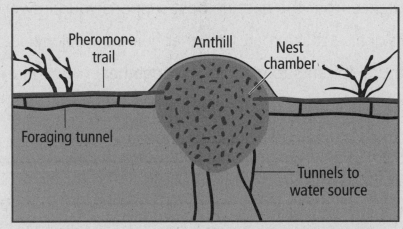

Ants travel along many different trails and tunnels.

Answer the following questions.

1 This question has two parts. First, answer Part A. Then, answer Part B.

Part A

What is the main idea of the text?

A. Ants live in colonies underground.

B. Ants spend most of their time foraging and looking for food.

C. Ants use chemical signals to keep from getting lost.

D. Ants live in anthills that have complex tunnels.

Part B

Which sentence from the passage **best** supports your answer in Part A?

A. These signals act like road signs that guide the colony.

B. It is natural for ants to want to stay together.

C. Many different trails and tunnels lead from these nests.

D. If the smell is weak, they look for another route.

> **Hint** The main idea is what the text is mostly about.

2 Explain how the diagram of the anthill helps you better understand the ideas in the text.

Write your answer on the lines below.

_____

_____

_____

> **Hint** Look at the details and labels in the diagram. What do they show?

3 Read these sentences from the text and the directions that follow.

Ants are always looking for food. Scouts head out first and leave a pheromone trail as they move toward the food sources they find. Then, other ants follow the trails to the food and bring it back to the nest. Because strong pheromone smells attract ants, they will follow them.

Circle the sentence that describes a cause and an effect.

> **Hint** A cause is something that happens. An effect is what happens as a result.

4 Read both parts of the question before responding.

Part A

Read the sentence from the article and the directions that follow.

Ants give off scents called <u>pheromones</u> that other ants follow.

What does the word <u>pheromones</u> mean?

A. chemical signals

B. trails, or paths

C. directions to follow

D. a kind of food

Part B

Which phrases from paragraph 3 of the text are context clues that explain the meaning of the word <u>pheromones</u>? Circle **all** that apply.

A. simple and amazing

B. give off scents

C. signals act like road signs

D. as a result

E. ants do not have noses

> **Hint** Reread the sentences in paragraph 3 before and after the first use of the word *pheromones* for context clues that explain what the word means.

Use the Reading Guide to help you understand the passage.

What Happens When an Ant Trail Is Blocked?

Reading Guide

Why do you think the author includes all the materials needed at the start of the experiment?

How does the author show steps in a process?

What is an important task in each step of the process?

A large number of ants will follow a single path to find food. What happens when that trail is blocked? In this experiment, you will safely disturb the ants' path and observe the results.

Materials

- food, such as honey or sugar
- wooden block
- measuring tape or ruler
- timer or watch
- notepad and pencil
- digital camera (optional)

Procedure

1. Find ants. Look for an anthill around patios or breaks in concrete.

2. Observe the ants for five minutes. Record what you see. Use words and drawings.

3. Place the food twenty-four inches away from the anthill. What do you think will happen? Observe and record again. Include drawings or photographs. Record how long it takes for things to happen. Count the number of ants you see at different times.

4. Give the ants time to form a trail to the food and back to the anthill. Observe what the ants do.

5. When the ants have formed a clear trail, block their path with the wooden block. (Be careful not to harm the ants.) Observe how the ants react to the block. Record your observations.

How does the student's drawing help you understand how ants act?

What do the student's observations tell you about the way ants act?

How does the conclusion answer the question asked at the beginning of the experiment?

6. Think about the results. What happened? How did ants react when their trail was blocked? Draw conclusions, and share your ideas with a partner.

Observe ants.		Block path.		Observe again.

Observations

One student did the experiment and wrote down what she saw. She also drew a picture of the ants walking.

Observations

Before Food Is Put Down	Before Blocking Path to Food	After Blocking Path
Four ants wandered out from the anthill. They wandered around and then went back in after two minutes.	About ten ants came out of the anthill. A few found the honey. They all went back to the anthill. Two minutes later, many ants came out. They walked in a line to the honey. They went back and forth to the anthill.	At first, the wooden block interrupted the line of ants. They wandered around for about ninety seconds. Then, a line formed again toward the honey.

Conclusions

Ants must follow smell rather than use sight to find food. At first, the wooden block confused the ants, and they lost track of the scent. They had a hard time seeing the food around the block. But the block could not stop the smell of the food or the pheromone trail. Once they found the smell, they went around or over the block to get to the honey.

Answer the following questions.

1 What is the text **mostly** about? What are the key details?
Write your answer on the lines below.

_____

_____

_____

_____

2 Match the graphic feature on the left with its purpose on the right.

A. flowchart

B. drawing

C. table

1. to identify materials needed

2. to show some steps in the process

3. to record observations

4. to block ants' path

5. to show how ants move

3 What did the student learn from this experiment?

A. Once ants lose their way, they cannot find a trail again.

B. Ants can follow a trail but have a bad sense of direction.

C. Ants need help to find food because they cannot do it themselves.

D. Ants can regain a path after it is interrupted.

4 Read both parts of the question before responding.

Part A

Reread the section "Procedure" from the text.

Which choice **best** describes how the paragraphs in that section are organized?

A. cause and effect

B. steps in a process

C. problem and solution

D. part to whole

Part B

What clues in the text help you identify your answer to Part A?

Write your answer on the lines below.

_____

_____

_____

_____

_____

5 The following steps from the experiment are out of order. In each box, write 2, 3, 4, or 5 so that the steps are in the correct order.

| 1 | Find an anthill. |

| | Place food twenty-four inches away from the anthill. Observe and record. |

| | Observe the ants for five minutes. Record observations. |

| | After the ants form a trail, block the path with a wooden block. Observe and record. |

| | Give the ants time to form a trail to the food and back to the anthill. |

| 6 | Think about your results and draw conclusions. |

6 What information is given in each section of the experiment? How do the sections connect to one another? Why was it important for the students to follow the steps in order?

Write your answers on the lines below.

_____

_____

_____

_____

_____

_____

_____

_____

_____

_____

_____

_____

_____

_____

RI.3.1, RI.3.2, RI.3.9, L.3.4

Analyze Informational Texts

1 GETTING THE IDEA

You read many kinds of texts at school. Sometimes, you read two or more texts on the same topic. This often happens when you are learning about real people, places, or things. The more you read about a topic, the more you learn.

Text Types and Text Structures

Different kinds of informational texts can have different text structures. The authors may also have different purposes for writing. Suppose you are learning about bears in class. You might read these types of texts.

- A science textbook may use a **part-to-whole** text structure to give basic information about a bear's body and its features.

- A magazine article may use **compare and contrast** to talk about different kinds of bears around the world.

- An opinion piece may use **problem and solution** to persuade you to help save bears or to help save a bear's habitat.

- A zoo Web site may use **sequence** to tell how one of its bears grew up from a cub or to tell how it spends its day.

- A brochure from a national park may use **steps in a process** to tell campers what they should do if they see a bear.

All these text types tell about bears, but they have different text structures. They may also have different main ideas and details or different points of view. It is important to be able to compare and contrast texts and to make connections between them.

Summarizing

Before you compare and contrast texts, look at the texts one at a time. Write a summary of each text in your own words. A good **summary** states the main idea and recounts the most important details. If the details happen in order, make sure to tell details in that same order. A good summary also shows that you understand what you have read.

Making Comparisons

Once you understand the texts, you are ready to make comparisons. When you **compare**, you tell how things are alike. When you **contrast**, you tell how things are different.

Read the two paragraphs. Circle the ways brown bears and polar bears are alike. Underline the ways they are different.

At one time, brown bears lived across much of the United States and as far south as Mexico. Now, they mostly live in the forests of Alaska and Canada. These large bears are sometimes called grizzly bears because of their coarse, brown fur. Brown bears eat grasses, roots, berries, insects, and fish. In winter, brown bears hibernate, or sleep, in a den. During that time, females may give birth to one to three cubs. In spring, the bears leave their winter dens to look for food. Mother bears care for their cubs for two years.

Polar bears are large bears that live in the Arctic. Polar bears are good swimmers. They hunt for seals in the icy waters and along the snowy coasts. Their thick white fur makes them hard to see in the snow. The fur also protects them from the cold. Females dig deep into the snow to make a den. They sleep most of the winter in the den and give birth to one or two cubs. The cubs stay with their mothers for a little over two years.

Making Connections

After you compare and contrast the texts, you can start to make connections between the facts and details you have read. Look at the chart to see the connections that one reader made.

Brown Bears	Both Bears	Polar Bears
• have coarse brown fur • live in Alaska and Canada • live in forests • eat grasses, roots, berries, insects, and fish	• are large • have fur • sleep in winter in a den • have cubs • care for cubs for two years	• have thick white fur • live in the snowy Arctic • hunt for seals • are good swimmers

You learned several things about brown bears and polar bears, but you also learned that the bears have a lot in common.

Language Spotlight • Multiple-Meaning Words

Multiple-meaning words have more than one meaning. Sometimes, you may read a word you know, but its meaning in a particular sentence isn't familiar. When this happens, use context clues to help you figure out the meaning of the word.

In each sentence below, the word <u>fly</u> has a different meaning. Draw a line from each sentence to the definition that tells how the word <u>fly</u> is used in the sentence.

Many birds <u>fly</u> south for the winter.

The <u>fly</u> buzzes around the food.

A pilot can <u>fly</u> a plane.

The batter hit a <u>fly</u> ball.

a winged insect

a baseball hit high into the air

to travel through the air

to operate an aircraft

Read the passage.

Learning to Be a Clown

In 1968, Ringling Brothers and Barnum & Bailey's Circus was facing a problem. The circus didn't have enough clowns. To make matters worse, the twelve clowns they did have were getting older. How long would the clowns still be able to travel with the circus?

Irvin Feld was one of the circus owners. He knew how important clowns were to the show. They made people laugh. They helped people relax from the stress of watching the other circus acts. They made people happy. Unlike other circus acts, the clowns focused on the audience and their feelings. Mr. Feld had an idea to solve the problem. He decided to start Ringling Brothers Clown College. The college was located in Venice, Florida, the winter home of the circus. Hundreds of people tried out for the college. But only thirty new clowns were accepted.

Clown College did not charge a fee to students. When Clown College first started, classes were six days a week and lasted for thirteen weeks. Students wore baggy pants and giant shoes to class. They learned to juggle, walk on stilts, and ride unicycles. They learned how to balance, to fall correctly, and to clown around. They even learned how to put on makeup and costumes.

For thirty years, Clown College held classes. The best students from each year were offered a job with the circus. Some graduates became clowns at other circuses. Others went on to entertain children in hospitals and schools.

By 1998, over a thousand clowns had completed Clown College. The circus now had plenty of clowns. Since Clown College was no longer needed, the directors decided to shut it down.

Luckily, that wasn't the end of Clown College. The circus decided to <u>train</u> clowns as it travels around the country. Some student clowns travel and learn with the circus. Others take classes in the cities the circus visits. The circus calls the new college "Clown College on the Road."

Answer the following questions.

1 Learning to become a clown takes physical skills. Support this statement with **two** details from the passage.

_____

_____

_____

_____

> **Hint** Find the part of the passage that talks about the different things clowns learn to do with their bodies. Look for details in that paragraph first. Think of action words as you look for details.

2 The following are events from the passage. In each box, write the numbers 2, 3, 4, or 5 so that the events are in the correct order.

| 1 | The Ringling Brothers and Barnum and Bailey's Circus was running out of clowns. |

| | After thirty years, the circus had more than enough clowns. |

| | Irwin Feld decided to start Clown College to solve the problem. |

| | At the college, students learned to juggle, walk on stilts, and ride a unicycle. |

| | Clown College decided to close in 1998. |

| 6 | The circus took Clown College on the road. |

> **Hint** Look for signal words in the passage to help you follow the order of events.

3 The following question has two parts. First, answer Part A. Then, answer Part B.

Part A

Why did Irvin Feld decide to start Clown College?

A. He wanted more clowns to visit hospitals.

B. He wanted to learn to be a clown.

C. He thought it would be funny to have a school for clowns.

D. He needed more clowns for his circus.

Part B

Underline **two** details from the passage that tell why clowns were important to the circus.

Hint Go back to the text and look for the problem that Irvin Feld faced to answer Part A. Read that paragraph again to find details to answer Part B.

4 Read the sentences from the passage and answer the question that follows.

Luckily, that wasn't the end of Clown College. The circus decided to <u>train</u> clowns as it travels around the country.

The word <u>train</u> is a multiple-meaning word. What is the meaning of the word <u>train</u> in the sentence?

A. a long line of moving people

B. a series of connected railroad cars that travel on a track

C. to teach someone how to do something

D. the part of a long dress that trails behind along the floor

Hint How is the word *train* used in the sentence? Does it name an object or is it an action word?

Use the Reading Guide to help you understand the passage.

Clowning Your Way to Good Health

Reading Guide

As you read, notice details in this passage that are not included in "Learning to Be a Clown." Also, think about ways the two passages are alike.

Why is becoming a clown a good combination of laughter and exercise?

What kind of physical activities do clowns learn to do?

How are clowns an important part of the community?

Have you ever heard the expression "Laughter is the best medicine"? Laughter, like exercise, reduces stress and increases your heart rate. So, what's the best way to combine laughter and exercise? Learn to be a clown.

Clowns have been making people laugh for years. One of the reasons clowns perform in a circus is to relieve the stress of the audience. For example, people become nervous while watching an acrobat flip through the air, and they get fearful when the lions perform. After each stressful act, the clowns come out. They put on skits. They ride giant unicycles or tiny tricycles. They have a great time. The people laugh. They are now relaxed and ready for the next exciting act.

Being a clown is also good exercise. Clown skills take a lot physical work. You need strong muscles to do the things these performers do with their bodies. Clowns run, leap, tumble, and stretch. They juggle and balance. They ride unicycles or walk on stilts. All of these activities are good exercise for the body. They are also good exercise for the mind. It takes a lot of concentration to be a good clown.

Clowns play an important part in the community. They visit people in hospitals and nursing homes. They perform at schools and parties. Their purpose is to make people happy. This is not just my opinion. For example, Irvin Feld, one of the owners of Ringling Brothers and Barnum & Bailey's Circus, felt so strongly about clowns that in 1968, he started a college where people train to become clowns.

Reading Guide

How is the job of a clown in a circus similar to the job of a clown visiting a hospital? How is it different?

What does the author mean by saying "clowning is also a big responsibility"?

Why do you think the author says, "Being a clown isn't for everyone"? What does the author suggest if you don't want to be a clown?

Clowns make people laugh, but clowning is also a big responsibility. Jokes and pranks are only funny if no one's feelings get hurt and if no one gets physically hurt. Learning to be a good clown helps you know the difference between good laughter and hurtful laughter. It helps you become a better person by learning to care about others.

The best way to learn to be a clown is to take clown classes. Many clowns offer clown classes in different parts of the country. Some of these clown teachers even learned their skills at the Ringling Brothers Clown College. Clown classes help people by providing plenty of exercise and laughter.

Being a clown isn't for everyone. But everyone should learn how to act like a clown. Laughter is good for the body and the mind. If more people laughed, the world would be a healthier, happier place.

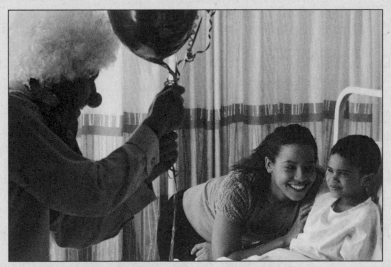

A visit from a clown can make a sick child and his family forget their troubles for a while.

Answer the following questions.

1 This question has two parts. First, answer Part A. Then, answer Part B.

Part A

What is the main idea of the passage?

A. "Laughter is the best medicine" is a true statement.

B. Laughter and exercise both reduce stress.

C. Being a clown improves your health through laughter and exercise.

D. You can take clown classes to learn how to be a clown.

Part B

Which sentences from the passage support your answer to Part A? Circle **all** that apply.

A. One of the reasons clowns perform in a circus is to relieve the stress of the audience.

B. Being a clown is also good exercise.

C. Clowns play an important part in the community.

D. Learning to be a good clown helps you know the difference between good laughter and hurtful laughter.

E. Laughter is good for the body and the mind.

2 How does the photograph and caption add to your understanding of the passage? Circle **all** that apply.

A. It shows how clowns visit hospitals to help patients feel better.

B. It shows that children sometimes have to stay in a hospital.

C. It shows that children and families enjoy clown visits.

D. It shows that clowns often have balloons.

Answer the following questions about both passages in this lesson.

3 This question has two parts. First, answer Part A. Then, answer Part B.

Part A

Read the paragraph below from "Learning to Be a Clown." Underline the details that tell what physical activities clowns learn to do.

> **Clown College did not charge a fee to students. When Clown College first started, classes were six days a week and lasted for thirteen weeks. Students wore baggy pants and giant shoes to class. They learned to juggle, walk on stilts, and ride unicycles. They learned how to balance, to fall correctly, and to clown around. They even learned how to put on makeup and costumes.**

Part B

What information from the passage "Clowning Your Way to Good Health" adds to your knowledge of the kinds of physical activities clowns do?

Write your answer on the lines below.

_____

_____

_____

_____

_____

4 Think about the main idea of "Learning to Be a Clown" and the main idea of "Clowning Your Way to Good Health." What is the purpose of each passage?

Write your answer on the lines below.

_____

_____

_____

_____

5 Read the following paragraphs from the passages and the directions that follow.

"Learning to Be a Clown"

For thirty years, Clown College held classes. The best clowns from each year were offered a job with the circus. Some graduates became clowns at other circuses. Others went on to entertain children in hospitals and schools.

"Clowning Your Way to Good Health"

Clowns play an important part in the community. They visit people in hospitals and nursing homes. They perform at schools and parties. Their purpose is to make people happy. This is not just my opinion. For example, Irvin Feld, one of the owners of Ringling Brothers and Barnum & Bailey's Circus, felt so strongly about clowns that in 1968, he started a college where people train to become clowns.

Underline the detail that is the same in both paragraphs.

6 You have read two nonfiction passages about clowns, "Learning to Be a Clown" and "Clowning Your Way to Good Health." Both passages mention the importance of the jobs clowns have.

Compare and contrast the passages to point out the most important points. Remember to use reasons and evidence from the passages in your response.

Write your answer on the lines below.

_____

_____

_____

_____

_____

_____

_____

_____

_____

_____

_____

_____

_____

_____

Analyze Texts Across Genres

1 GETTING THE IDEA

Authors may write about one topic in many different ways. Think about the topic of the rain forest. One author may write an informational text to give facts about the rain forest. Another may write a realistic fiction story about a family who visits a rain forest.

Fiction and Nonfiction

Fiction is writing that is made up by the author. **Nonfiction** presents facts and other information based on real life. Look at the chart below to compare and contrast the two types of texts.

Fiction	Both	Nonfiction
• tells a story that is made up by the author • can be based on events from real life	• may present information in the form of a story • are told from a certain point of view • can include scientific or historical information	• gives facts to support a main idea • may tell a true story • may be broken into sections with headings

Fiction includes fables, folktales, and myths. Some nonfiction texts are newspaper articles, science experiments, and biographies. Each type of text has specific traits. Some text types include elements of fiction and nonfiction.

Historical fiction is set in a real time or place from the past. For example, a made-up story about life in the 1800s is historical fiction. While these stories may include real people and events, they also have characters, events, and dialogue that are made up.

Realistic fiction also uses settings that may seem real, such as a mall or a school. However, authors make up the details in realistic fiction. They write about the events and characters in a way that makes them seem real.

Analyze Texts

When you read two related texts, pay attention to the main ideas and details. Ask questions as you read each text. This will help you compare and contrast the texts later.

Fiction	Nonfiction
What is the main message, or theme, of the story?	What is the main idea of the text?
Who are the characters? What is the setting? What are the key events?	What supporting details does the author include?

The main message of a story is not always directly stated. You may have to figure it out. The main idea of a nonfiction article is easier to identify. Once you know the main idea and details of each text, you can figure out what the texts have in common.

Read the fiction and nonfiction passages that follow. Pay attention to the details and figure out the main point each author is trying to convey. Then, circle any elements that are alike. Underline any elements that are different.

Bertha and the Spider

Bertha the cow watched as a spider weaved its silky thread between the tree and the barn. She stared in amazement as a beautiful web took shape.

Bertha couldn't help but feel jealous. The spider could walk across the air on its special silk and catch its own food. Most importantly, the humans never noticed it. All Bertha could do was walk around the field, eat grass, and give milk.

Ah well, Bertha thought as she lay down. *I guess I will just have to settle for being a cow.*

How Spiders Trap Food

Many spiders use webs to trap their food. They use the special silk inside their bodies to make their webs. A spider makes part of its web sticky so it can trap insects. But it leaves part of the web smooth so it can move around without getting stuck.

Although a spider does not have very good eyesight, it has a strong sense of touch. A spider often sits in its web and waits. When an insect hits the web, the spider feels the movement. Then, it snatches up its meal.

Now, compare and contrast the two passages. Use a Venn diagram to organize your ideas.

"Bertha and the Spider"   **Both**   **"How Spiders Trap Food"**

- fiction story of a cow who is jealous of a spider
- gives the character's thoughts about a spider

- have similar topic: spiders and their webs
- use details to describe how a spider makes its web

- informational text about how spiders build webs to trap insects
- gives facts as supporting details

Language Spotlight • Synonyms

Synonyms are words with almost the same meaning. For example, the words *think*, *ponder*, and *imagine* each relate to how people consider ideas. But each one means something slightly different. Read this sentence from "Bertha and the Spider."

Most importantly, the humans never <u>noticed</u> it.

Circle the words below that are similar to the word *noticed*.

observed   ignored   needed   viewed   saw

Read the passage.

What Does a Seed Need to Grow?

Plants grow from seeds. For a seed to <u>germinate</u>, it needs light, air, and water. The experiment below can help you meet the needs of a seed. Follow the steps correctly, and the seeds will germinate!

Materials

- a few seeds of any type, as fresh as possible
- a paper towel
- a plastic bag with zipper at top
- a stapler
- a half cup of water

Steps to Follow

1. Fold the paper towel until it is smaller than the plastic bag.

2. Put the paper towel in the plastic bag.

3. Measure three inches from the top of the bag. Staple through the bag and paper towel. Make a line of staples across the bag. This area is where the seeds will sit.

4. Pour water into the bag. The paper towel should soak up most of the water. Leave a little bit of extra water in the bag.

5. Place the seeds in the bag. They should sit above the line of staples.

6. Seal the bag so no air gets in. Then tape the bag to a window that gets sunlight.

7. Watch your seeds. After a few days, you should start to see roots. This means the seed has germinated and your experiment was a success!

Now, you can move your seeds. Plant them in a pot or in the ground. Soil will give them the nutrients they need to grow.

What might happen if the seeds do not get all their needs met? You can change this experiment to find out. Try one of these changes to learn more:

- Place one bag of seeds in a dark area. Compare it to one that was placed in sunlight.
- Do not use water in one bag of seeds. Compare it to a bag that did get water.
- Do not seal one bag of seeds. Compare it to a bag that you did seal.

Answer the following questions.

1 These steps from the experiment are out of order. Write numbers 1 through 5 in the boxes to put the steps in the correct order.

☐ Put the seeds in the bag.

☐ Add water to the bag.

☐ Tape the bag to a window.

☐ Staple a line across the top of the bag, three inches down from the top.

☐ Insert a folded paper towel into the bag.

Hint Look at the numbered list in the passage. What has to happen first? Which is the last step to complete?

2 Which sentence **best** tells the main idea of this text?

A. Experiments can help you learn about science.

B. Plants need water to live.

C. Stapling the plastic bag will make a place for the seeds to sit.

D. Plants must have certain needs met in order to live and grow.

E. Seeds should be placed near a window to get sunlight.

F. You should follow the steps of an experiment in order.

Hint Think about what the text is mostly about. What does the author want you to learn from the experiment?

3 The following question has two parts. First, answer Part A. Then, answer Part B.

Part A

Read this sentence from the passage and the question that follows.

> **For a seed to germinate, it needs light, air, and water.**

What does the word germinate mean in the sentence?

A. to produce a seed

B. to sprout

C. to shrivel up and die

D. to make new plants

Part B

Which sentence from the passage includes a word with a similar meaning to germinate?

A. Plants grow from seeds.

B. First, fold a paper towel until it is smaller than the plastic bag.

C. After a few days, you should start to see roots.

D. Plant them in a pot or in the ground.

Hint First, identify the meaning of the word *germinate*. What do light, air, and water help the seed do? Use your understanding of *germinate* to choose your answer to Part B.

4 Why does the author suggest changes that can be made to the experiment? Use evidence from the text to support your answer.

Write your answer on the lines below.

_____

_____

_____

_____

Use the Reading Guide to help you understand the passage.

Amy's Blue-Ribbon Project

Reading Guide

What type of text is this? How can you tell?

Why does Amy want to do something special for her science experiment?

What might happen if Amy doesn't follow all the steps of the experiment?

Billy and his younger sister, Amy, were sitting at the kitchen table, talking about science projects. "Everyone does the seeds in the bag experiment. You have to put a twist on it if you want to win the blue ribbon," Billy told Amy.

"Like what?" she asked him.

"It's your experiment. You decide."

Amy's teacher, Mrs. Garcia, had suggested the experiment. She knew that Amy loved flowers. On many days, Amy would bring her teacher a bright bloom. Just yesterday, she brought in a bunch of purple asters. They were her favorite.

Amy wanted to impress the judges at the science fair. She knew that it would take something special to win first prize. She pictured herself holding the blue ribbon up to the cheering crowd. She couldn't help but smile at the thought. Unlike Billy, she didn't have shelves of soccer trophies to show off. She was more of a bookworm than an athlete. But this would be her time to shine. Her parents would be so proud.

She thought that Billy might be right, though. To do the seed experiment, she would need a twist to make it new and different. It was the only way she could beat her classmates. She knew they all had secrets up their sleeves. Leo was planning an exploding volcano. Sophia was training her pet mice to run through a maze.

Up in her room, Amy gathered her materials. She needed a paper towel, water, seeds, and a plastic bag. Then, she read through the directions. *Why do I need a paper towel?* she pondered. *Can't the seeds just get the water from what I pour in the bag?*

So, she stapled the bag and poured water to the stapled line. Then she added in her seeds. Next was the hard part—waiting. Patience wasn't Amy's best skill. She paced back in forth in front of the bag of seeds, waiting and watching. Nothing happened.

Finally, after four days, she decided the experiment did not work. She put her head down on her desk. She wondered if she should give up on the idea of a blue ribbon.

Then, Billy poked his head in her room.

"Why so glum, sis?" he asked, nudging her.

"Because my experiment is a dud. Look at my seeds. I don't see any roots or stems. Do you?"

"Nope, but that doesn't mean you should quit. Coach always tells us the shot you don't take could win the game. Why don't you read the instructions again?"

Amy looked at the paper on her desk. Perhaps the paper towel was more important than she thought. She picked up the paper and turned it over. Suddenly, she realized there were more steps she hadn't seen before. She was supposed to tape the bag to a window! Her bag was sitting on her desk. And her room was dark.

"I think I have my twist!" she shouted.

Billy looked at her sideways. "Your twist is that you didn't read all the directions?"

"No, silly. I can do the experiment again and compare the two versions. I can compare and contrast what happens when a seed doesn't get everything it needs. I can even use my own mistake to tell about the importance of following directions in order. The teachers will like that, for sure! They are always telling us to be more careful when we read directions."

Billy laughed. "Sounds like a fortunate discovery to me! And it's a science lesson people will want to remember. Now, we just have to find the perfect place to hang your blue ribbon."

Answer the following questions.

1 This question has two parts. First, answer Part A. Then, answer Part B.

Part A

What type of text is "Amy's Blue-Ribbon Project"?

A. fable

B. biography

C. informational text

D. realistic fiction

E. myth

Part B

Which clues help you to answer Part A? Choose **all** that apply.

A. The author presents facts about seeds.

B. The events could actually happen in real life.

C. The text lists steps in the order you should follow them.

D. The characters were made up by the author.

E. The events are set in a real time from the past.

2 Read the sentence from the passage below, and answer the question that follows.

She paced back in forth in front of the bag of seeds, waiting and watching.

Why does the author use the word paced to describe how Amy walks?

A. to show that Amy is running quickly across the room

B. to show that Amy is crawling on the ground in front of the seeds

C. to show that Amy is eager for something to happen

D. to show how Amy looks at the seeds

Answer the following questions about both passages in this lesson.

3 Which statement is an important idea in **both** "What Does a Seed Need to Grow?" and "Amy's Blue-Ribbon Project"?

A. Science experiments often include a list of materials and steps to follow.

B. Seeds need certain things in order to live and grow.

C. Many students have tried the seeds-in-a-bag experiment.

D. Don't give up on something too quickly.

E. Many people, such as Amy, love flowers.

4 Which details from "What Does a Seed Need to Grow?" relate to the "twist" in Amy's experiment? Choose **all** that apply.

A. Follow the steps correctly, and the seeds will germinate!

B. Seal the bag so no air gets in.

C. Measure three inches from the top of the bag.

D. Place the seeds in the bag.

E. Now, you can move your seeds. Plant them in a pot or in the ground.

F. Place one bag of seeds in a dark area. Compare it to the one that was placed in sunlight.

5 The following question has two parts. First, answer Part A. Then, answer Part B.

Part A

Which parts of the science experiment did Amy do differently?

A. She didn't use a paper towel in the bag or tape the bag to a window.

B. She didn't use enough seeds or put the seeds in a bag.

C. She didn't put water in the bag or tape the bag to a window.

D. She didn't watch the seeds to see if they grew roots or stems.

Part B

Use your answer from Part A to explain why Amy's seeds did not grow well the first time she tried the experiment.

Write your answer on the lines below.

_____

_____

_____

_____

6 "What Does a Seed Need to Grow?" and "Amy's Blue-Ribbon Project" both relate to a science experiment about growing seeds in a bag. Compare and contrast the main message or idea of each text and the details used in each one.

Write your answer on the lines below.

_____

_____

_____

_____

_____

_____

_____

_____

_____

_____

_____

_____

_____

_____

Read the passage.

The Zoetrope

Have you ever wondered how movies were invented? Would you believe that a simple toy was an important part of the story? In 1834, a man named William Horner invented an unusual toy. People later called the toy a zoetrope (**zoh**-ee-trohp).

How a Zoetrope Works

A zoetrope looks a lot like a merry-go-round. It is a cylinder that spins. But it does not have animals you can ride. No music plays. The cylinder in a zoetrope is hollow. The outside of the cylinder has slits cut in it, while the inside has many pictures drawn on it. The pictures are not the same. Each picture is a tiny bit different. The pictures are arranged in a certain order.

Take a look at the zoetrope below. You can see that the pictures inside show a horse that is running. When the zoetrope spins, something interesting happens. A person can see the pictures through the slits on the outside. But the narrow slits do not let a person see each picture for very long. Also, the pictures move very quickly. The brain cannot see each picture separately. Instead, the brain blends them into a moving picture. The faster the zoetrope spins, the smoother the pictures move.

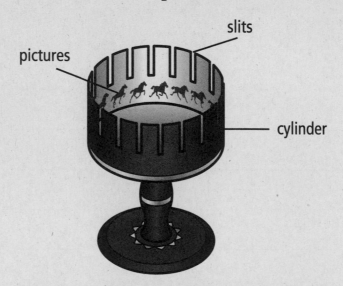

slits

pictures

cylinder

This is a zoetrope. Look closely at the pictures.
Each horse is slightly different from the one before it.
As the cylinder spins, you think you are seeing one
horse running.

The Zoetrope Leads to Modern Movies

Years later, a similar toy was invented. Like the zoetrope, it had pictures and spun around. But this toy had mirrors instead of slits. People saw the pictures reflected in the mirrors.

As time went on, more improvements were made to the toy. People realized it could be attached to a projector. This is a machine that shines light through a magnifying glass. The machine uses the light to <u>project</u> the moving pictures from the toy, similar to the way the sun projects your shadow. Soon, plastic film was invented. It replaced the spinning cylinder. Light passed through the film, and the film moved quickly through the projector. An image was projected onto a screen. Modern movies were born!

Many of today's movies are projected digitally using computers. But some movies still are shown on film that is passed through a projector. The long strip of plastic film is filled with a series of squares. These squares are called frames. Each frame holds one picture. Each picture differs a tiny bit from the picture before it. When the piece of film slides through a movie projector, the pictures flash on the screen very quickly. The pictures move too fast for our eyes to see each frame alone. Instead, our brain blends them into a moving picture, just the way it does with pictures on a zoetrope.

Modern Zoetropes

Zoetropes are not common toys anymore. Most kids do not own one. However, people can still see them in interesting places. Zoetropes are now often created by artists. Some artists make zoetropes that take up entire rooms! You can sometimes see these zoetropes in museums.

In cities like New York, you can also see zoetropes on tunnel walls. Instead of a cylinder, the zoetrope is flat. The flat zoetrope also has many slits. Pictures are behind the slits. When a subway train moves past, people inside the train see a very short movie through the slits. It is another way people have fun with zoetropes.

Answer the following questions.

1 Reread paragraph 3 of the passage. Then read the sentences from the paragraph below.

But the narrow slits do not let a person see each picture for very long.
The faster the zoetrope spins, the smoother the pictures move.
When the zoetrope spins, something interesting happens.
Instead, the brain blends them into a moving picture.

Complete the web below. Write the sentence that tells the main idea in the big oval. Write the sentences that give supporting details in the small ovals.

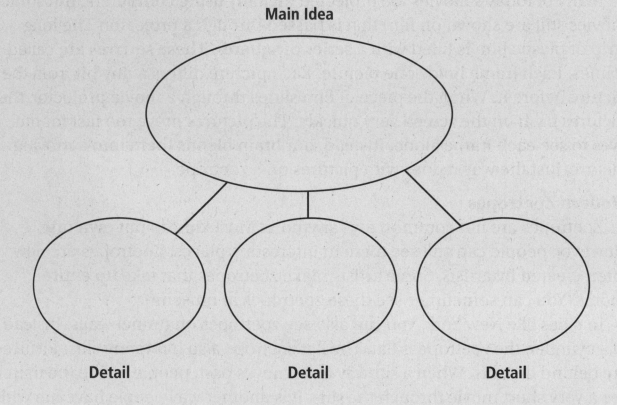

2 The following question has two parts. First, answer Part A. Then, answer Part B.

Part A

Read these sentences from the passage.

> **As time went on, more improvements were made to the toy. People realized it could be attached to a projector. This is a machine that shines light through a magnifying glass. The machine uses the light to <u>project</u> the moving pictures from the toy, similar to the way the sun projects your shadow.**

What is the meaning of the word <u>project</u> as it is used in the sentence?

A. complete an assignment

B. speak loudly

C. guess

D. throw outward

Part B

Write a sentence that uses <u>project</u> in the same way it is used in Part A.

_____

_____

3 The following question has two parts. First, answer Part A. Then, answer Part B.

Part A

Circle the text features below that are used in the passage.

caption	key word
heading	sidebar

Part B

Choose a text feature you circled in Part A. Explain one way it helps you understand an idea in the passage.

_____

_____

4 Circle the heading you would look under to find information about how the zoetrope is used today.

How a Zoetrope Works
Modern Zoetropes
The Zoetrope Leads to Modern Movies

5 The following question has two parts. First, answer Part A. Then, answer Part B.

Part A

Read this paragraph from the passage.

> **Years later, a similar toy was invented. Like the zoetrope, it had pictures and spun around. But this toy had mirrors instead of slits. People saw the pictures reflected in the mirrors.**

Which **best** describes how the sentences in the paragraph are organized?

A. cause and effect

B. sequence

C. compare and contrast

D. problem and solution

Part B

Underline **two** signal words in the paragraph that helped you identify its structure.

Read the passage.

Build Your Own Zoetrope

A zoetrope is a toy that plays a trick on your brain. When you look through a spinning zoetrope, the pictures inside seem to move.

It is easy to build a zoetrope. You can use items you have around your house. However, you will need an adult to help with some steps.

Materials

42-ounce round cardboard oatmeal container

scissors

ruler

black paint

white paper, 16 inches long by

2 inches wide

black marker

colored pencil, white or yellow

sharpened pencil

modeling clay

empty spool of thread

Directions

1. Use the scissors to cut the container in half. Ask an adult to help with this step. Save the bottom of the container. Recycle the other half.

2. Paint the outside and the inside of the container with black paint. Set the container aside to dry.

3. After the paint is dry, use the ruler and colored pencil to mark the top of the container. Make twelve marks around the edge. Space them evenly, like the numbers on a clock.

4. Use the ruler and colored pencil to draw twelve rectangles down the side of the container. Begin each line at the mark you made on the top of the container. Make each rectangle two inches long and about one-eighth inch wide. When you are done, the container should look like the drawing in Figure 1.

Figure 1

5. Cut out the rectangles you drew. This will make slits. Ask an adult to help with this step.

6. Next, use the pointy end of the pencil to make a hole in the center of the container's base. Push the pencil most of the way through. Ask an adult to help with this step.

7. Make sure the eraser end of the pencil is inside the container.

8. Now, slide the empty spool of thread onto the pencil. Push the spool until it is just below the container. Then, put a lump of clay under the spool to hold it in place.

9. Try spinning the zoetrope. If it wobbles, add some clay to the top of the pencil.

10. Use the ruler to divide the piece of paper into twelve equal boxes. To do this, measure one and three-eighth inches from the end. Draw a line. Measure another one and three-eighth inches. Draw another line. Continue until your paper is marked as shown in Figure 2.

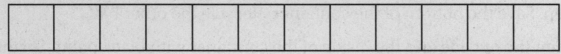

Figure 2

11. Use the black marker to draw a picture in each box. Make the pictures similar. But make sure each has a tiny change. Figure 3 shows an example. Each picture of the sun is slightly different from the one before it.

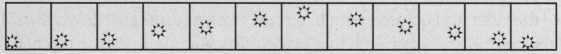

Figure 3

12. Tape your drawing inside the zoetrope. Make sure to line it up so that each picture is across from a slit.

13. Your zoetrope is ready! Spin the zoetrope slowly. Then spin it quickly. How does the movie change? If you used the pictures from Figure 3, you will see the sun rising and setting.

14. You can change the pictures in your zoetrope whenever you like.

Answer the following questions.

6 This question has two parts. First, answer Part A. Then, answer Part B.

Part A

Read these paragraphs from "Build Your Own Zoetrope" below. Underline a detail that describes the author's opinion about building a zoetrope.

> **A zoetrope is a toy that plays a trick on your brain. When you look through a spinning zoetrope, the pictures inside seem to move.**
>
> **It is easy to build a zoetrope. You can use items you have around your house. However, you will need an adult to help with some steps.**

Part B

What is one reason the author includes to support the opinion you identified in Part A? Write the reason on the lines below.

_____

_____

7 How do the diagrams in "Build Your Own Zoetrope" help you better understand how to make a zoetrope? Choose **all** that apply.

A. They show what a finished zoetrope looks like.

B. They describe how to spin a zoetrope.

C. They show what different parts of a zoetrope look like.

D. They give more information about some steps in the process.

E. They tell what you need to make a zoetrope.

8 Some of the steps to build a zoetrope are shown below, but they are out of order. Write 2, 3, 4, or 5 in each box to put the steps in the correct order.

1	Paint the outside and the inside of the container with black paint.
	Make each rectangle two inches long and about one-eighth inch wide.
	Slide the empty spool of thread onto the pencil.
	Set the container aside to dry.
	Make twelve marks around the edge.
6	Use a black marker to draw a picture in each box.

9 Which detail could **best** be added to step 5 to make the directions clearer?

A. You will be able to see the black inside the container.

B. Do not do step 6 before this step.

C. The slits should not be shaped like circles.

D. Remember that each slit should be the same width.

PERFORMANCE TASK

You have read two passages about zoetropes. The first passage gives information about how zoetropes work. The second passage tells how to build a zoetrope. Describe **three** ways that the information in the first passage helps you to understand the steps listed in the second passage. Support your response with reasons and evidence from both passages.

Write your answer on the lines below.

_____

_____

_____

_____

_____

_____

_____

_____

_____

_____

_____

_____

_____

_____

_____

STRAND
3

Writing

W.3.1.a–d, W.3.2.a–d, W.3.3.a, W.3.3.c, W.3.3.d, W.3.4, W.3.5, L.3.1.h

Writing Foundations

① GETTING THE IDEA

In school, you write different kinds of texts—stories, reports, or opinions. No matter what you write, there are five steps you can follow to make your final piece the best it can be. These steps are called the "writing process." The five steps are prewriting, writing, revising, editing, and publishing.

Prewriting

The first step in the writing process is prewriting. **Prewriting** is when you decide on a topic and on what you want to say about it. The **topic** is the subject of a text.

Choosing a Topic Choose a topic that is not too big and not too small. For example, the topic "Famous Buildings" is too big. There are too many famous buildings to write about. The topic "Height of the Empire State Building" is too small. You could write about this topic in just a few sentences. The topic "Empire State Building" is a good topic. It is not too big or too small.

Use a graphic organizer to plan what you want to say about your topic. Look at the web below. How does asking questions help you figure out what to include? Underline the topic, and draw an arrow from the topic to each question.

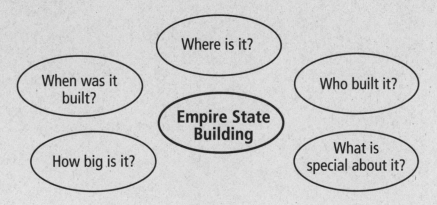

Deciding on a Task and Purpose Prewriting is also when you decide on your task and purpose. The **purpose** is the reason for writing. Here are some kinds of writing tasks and their purposes. Keep your task and purpose in mind throughout the writing process.

Task	Purpose
opinion piece	to state an opinion on a topic and give reasons to convince readers to think the same way or to take action
informational text	to inform readers about a topic using facts, examples, and other details that support the main idea
narrative	to entertain readers with a story about real or made-up characters and events

Planning a Narrative A **narrative** is a story. Every good story has a beginning, a middle, and an end. The beginning introduces the **characters** (the people or animals in your story), the **setting** (where and when the story takes place), and the problem to be solved. The middle of the story tells what the characters do to solve the problem. Most of the **plot**, or story events, happen in the middle. The end of the story is the **resolution**, or how the characters solve the problem.

You can use a flowchart like the one below to help you plan your story.

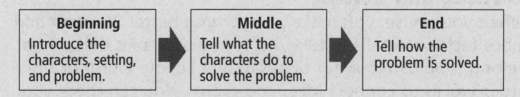

Beginning	**Middle**	**End**
Introduce the characters, setting, and problem.	Tell what the characters do to solve the problem.	Tell how the problem is solved.

Planning Informational Texts and Opinion Pieces

Informational texts and **opinion pieces** also have a beginning, a middle, and an end. In the beginning, state the main idea or opinion. In the middle, give reasons or evidence to support the main idea or opinion. At the end, state the main idea or opinion again. You can use a graphic organizer like this one to help you plan your writing.

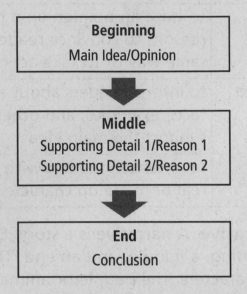

Beginning
Main Idea/Opinion

Middle
Supporting Detail 1/Reason 1
Supporting Detail 2/Reason 2

End
Conclusion

Writing

The second step in the writing process is writing. **Writing** is getting your ideas down on paper. This is called a **first draft**. In a first draft, you will probably make mistakes. That's OK. It is more important to get your ideas down first and fix mistakes later. Sometimes, you may not have time to rewrite your draft. So follow your writing plan closely and write neatly.

Revising and Editing

When you **revise**, you make your writing better. You can add more facts or details or take out facts and details that do not belong. You can look for places to add linking words or time-order words to connect ideas and events. You can check your word choices to be sure you have expressed your ideas clearly. If possible, ask a classmate to read your draft and suggest ways to improve it.

When you **edit**, you correct mistakes in spelling, grammar, capitalization, and punctuation. If you think a word may not be spelled correctly, check the spelling in a dictionary. Reread your work a few times. Does anything *sound* wrong? Doing this will help you spot common errors in grammar.

Reviewing Your Work Sometimes, you may have to revise and edit in the same step. Use this checklist to help you.

- ☐ Do I state my main idea or opinion clearly?
- ☐ Do I use enough details or reasons to support my main idea or opinion?
- ☐ Do I present my ideas in a way that makes sense?
- ☐ Do I express my ideas clearly?
- ☐ Does my writing have a clear beginning and ending?
- ☐ Is my writing free of grammar, spelling, capitalization, and punctuation errors?

Publishing

The last step is publishing. **Publishing** is making a final copy of your writing. You can either write it neatly on lined paper or use a computer to write it. The final copy should include all the changes you made in the revising and editing steps.

Language Spotlight • Conjunctions

A **conjunction** is a word, such as *and, or, but,* or *so,* that joins other words or groups of words. Using conjunctions in your writing helps you connect ideas. Read the following sentences. The underlined words are conjunctions. What two ideas does each connect? Circle the parts of each sentence that the conjunction connects.

Jack <u>and</u> Jill rode the elevator to the top of the building.

Jack enjoyed the ride, <u>but</u> Jill did not.

Will the twins enjoy the view, <u>or</u> won't they?

Read the passage.

A Visit to the Space Needle

Paulo grasped his grandmother's hand as his older sister Belen ran ahead.

"Hurry up," Belen called. "I can't wait to get to the top of the Space Needle."

Paulo looked worried. "Don't worry," said Grandma. "It's perfectly safe. Over a million people go to the top of the Space Needle every year."

"Why?" asked Paulo. "What's so special about it?"

"Well," Grandma explained, "there's a beautiful view of the city of Seattle from the top, and it's very historic."

"What makes it historic?" asked Belen.

"I remember when it was being built in 1961. I was going to college here at the time. It was the centerpiece of the 1962 World's Fair."

"You mean like an amusement park?" Paolo asked. Suddenly, he looked interested.

"There were some rides at the World's Fair, but it was mainly to celebrate science and the future," answered Grandma. "They called it 'Century 21.'"

Grandma bought tickets at the window. "Whew!" she said. "Prices sure have gone up. Back in 1962, it cost only one dollar to ride to the top."

Belen read from the information brochure. "It says here that almost 12,000 people a day rode the Space Needle during the fair. It also says the needle is 605 feet high!"

"It used to be the tallest building west of the Mississippi," Grandma added.

Paulo hesitated at the door of the outside elevator. "Is this safe?"

"Of course, it's safe," Belen said. "I just read that each elevator has seven cables, even though it needs only one."

Grandma guided the children onto the elevator and watched as they looked excitedly out the window. Forty-three seconds later, the elevator stopped 520 feet from the ground.

"Walk. Don't run!" Grandma warned as Paulo and Belen stepped onto the observation deck. Grandma followed behind the children as they went from one window to another.

Grandma looked in amazement at the safety grid around the platform. She didn't want to tell the children that the observation deck used to be strictly open air with only a handrail to keep people from falling over the side.

"What's that water over there?" asked Paulo.

Belen was quick to answer. "It's Puget Sound. I read about it in school."

"That's right!" smiled Grandma. "And for being so smart, I think I'll take you to Sky City, the revolving restaurant, for a snack when we're done here. We might even go to the Space Base to get some souvenirs."

Paulo and Belen both grinned from ear to ear.

Answer the following questions.

1 This question has two parts. First, answer Part A. Then, answer Part B.

Part A

Match each character on the left with what he or she said on the right.

A. Grandma		**1.** "Is this safe?"	
B. Belen		**2.** "Prices sure have gone up."	
C. Paulo		**3.** "It's Puget Sound. I read about it in school."	

Part B

Write one sentence about each character. Tell what he or she is like based on your answers to Part A.

Write your sentences on the lines below.

_____

_____

_____

_____

> **Hint** Consider what you learn about the characters from what they say.

2 Read the paragraph from the passage and the directions that follow.

> **"There were some rides at the World's Fair, but it was mainly to celebrate science and the future," answered Grandma. "They called it 'Century 21.'"**

Circle **two** conjunctions in the paragraph.

> **Hint** A conjunction is a word that connects words or ideas in a sentence.

3 The following question has two parts. First, answer Part A. Then, answer Part B.

Part A

What was the author's purpose for writing "A Visit to the Space Needle"?

A. to explain how the Space Needle was built

B. to inform readers about facts about the 1962 World's Fair

C. to narrate a story about a visit to the Space Needle

D. to persuade readers to visit the Space Needle

Part B

Explain why you chose your answer in Part A. Write your response on the lines below.

_____

_____

_____

_____

Hint Think about what happened in the passage. How does this relate to the author's purpose?

4 The following question has two parts. First, answer Part A. Then, answer Part B.

Part A

Which of the following characters was fearful about visiting the Space Needle?

A. Grandma

B. Belen

C. Paulo

D. None of the above

Part B

Underline **two** sentences from the passage that support your answer to Part A.

Hint Think about each character's traits, or qualities. Part A asks you to identify the character who was fearful. To answer Part B, think about what the character did to show he or she was fearful.

5 How did the author organize events in this passage?

A. in sequence with dialogue that shows what the characters do

B. with causes and effects that explain why the Space Needle was built

C. with paragraphs that tell an opinion about the Space Needle and reasons for the opinion

D. with descriptive paragraphs that provide details about what the Space Needle looks like

Hint Think about what you know about narratives and how they are organized. What clues can you use to tell how this passage is organized?

Use the Reading Guide to help you understand the passage.

From Doodle to Icon

Reading Guide

Why was the Space Needle built in Seattle?

How was the needle built?

What was the author's purpose for writing this passage? How do you know?

The Space Needle in Seattle, Washington, is like the Eiffel Tower in Paris, France, in some ways. Both are icons, or symbols, for their cities. And both were built for World's Fairs.

A Big Idea

Seattle was chosen to host the 1962 World's Fair. It was a big deal. A man named Edward Carlson became chairman of the fair. On a trip to Germany, he had seen the Stuttgart Tower. It had a restaurant and an observation deck. Stuttgart Tower gave Carlson an idea. He drew his idea on a paper placemat. That doodle became the idea for the design of the Space Needle. The design was approved just eighteen months before the fair was to open.

Seattle had to move fast to get everything done on time. The planners had no permits, no money, and no place to build. Five men came to the rescue. They paid for the land and the construction.

The Work Begins

Work on the Space Needle began just one year before the fair's opening. Workers used no nets, harnesses, or other safety gear during construction. Fortunately, no one was killed. It's hard to believe that the 605-foot tower was built in such a short time.

The elevators were unique for 1962. They were on the outside of the tower and had windows. The last elevator was put in place the day before the fair opened.

Even though the needle was built quickly, it was built to be safe. It can take winds up to 200 miles per hour. A major earthquake won't knock it down. Twenty-five lightning rods on the roof protect it from lightning. In addition, the elevators slow down in high winds. Each one has seven cables, although one could do the job. If all seven cables broke, a special brake would lock the elevator in place.

The Space Needle has a revolving restaurant 500 feet above the ground. It was only the second revolving restaurant in the world in 1962. The whole restaurant does not go around. Only the floor next to the windows moves around in a circle. The people sitting by the windows have a changing view. The restaurant was called the Eye of the Needle.

Changes

For its anniversary in 1982, the Space Needle made some changes. The revolving restaurant and the top level were redone. The biggest change was the addition of the SkyLine Level. It was part of the original design but wasn't built until twenty years later. The SkyLine Level is a restaurant for large groups of people. It is 100 feet above the ground.

In 1992, Seattle celebrated the New Year with fireworks from atop the Space Needle. The event was so popular that it has become a yearly tradition.

More changes came in 2000. The revolving restaurant got a new design and a new name: Sky City. The observation deck was redone. Outside lights were added. A pavilion was built. A store called Space Base was also built. Even the needle got a new paint job.

Since it was built in 1962, Seattle's Space Needle has been a popular attraction. Although it has changed a great deal over the years, it is still an icon.

Answer the following questions.

1 Read both parts of the question before responding.

Part A

Which **two** statements support the idea that the Space Needle was built to be safe?

A. The Space Needle was built to withstand winds up to 200 miles per hour and a major earthquake.

B. No safety gear, such as nets or harnesses, were used by construction workers.

C. Five men came to the rescue by paying cash for the property and the construction.

D. Twenty-five lightning rods on the roof protect the needle from lightning.

Part B

Underline the details from the passage that support the idea that the elevators were also built to be safe.

2 Read the following paragraph from the passage. Circle **two** conjunctions.

> **For its anniversary in 1982, the Space Needle made some changes. The revolving restaurant and the top level were redone. The biggest change was the addition of the SkyLine Level. It was part of the original design but wasn't built until twenty years later. The SkyLine Level is a restaurant for large groups of people. It is 100 feet above the ground.**

3 Read the list of words and phrases that describe Sky City or the SkyLine Level. Then, follow the directions below.

> **built in 1962**
>
> **built in 1982**
>
> **restaurant**
>
> **revolves**
>
> **serves large groups of people**
>
> **built far above the ground**

Write the words and phrases from the list in the correct places in the chart. Some words describe both Sky City and the SkyLine Level. Write those in the middle.

Sky City	Both	SkyLine Level

4 Reread the conclusion of the passage in the last paragraph. Which of the following sentences could be added to make the conclusion stronger?

A. The men who provided money to build the Space Needle should be congratulated.

B. Seattle will continue to improve the Space Needle.

C. It remains a symbol of hope for the future.

D. The SkyLine Level is a good place for a wedding.

5 In "A Visit to the Space Needle," you read about a family's visit to that place. In "From Doodle to Icon," you read about why the Space Needle was built and how it has changed over the years. Write a letter to persuade a friend to visit the Space Needle. Use reasons, facts, and details from both passages to support your point of view.

Use the writing process to plan, write, revise, and edit your letter. Be sure to include a beginning, middle, and end. You may plan your letter in the space below. Write your letter on the following pages.

Plan

Write your letter on the lines below.

_____

_____

_____

_____

_____

_____

_____

_____

_____

_____

_____

_____

_____

_____

_____

_____

Write about Texts

1 GETTING THE IDEA

When you talk about a story that you have read, you often share how you feel about the characters, the setting, or the plot. You can also share your ideas about a story in writing.

Understanding a Prompt

Sometimes, you will be asked to respond to a writing prompt. A **writing prompt** asks a question about a text you have read. Read this example. Circle the title of the text. Then, underline the question you need to answer.

> In "The Grasshopper and the Ant," the grasshopper and the ant disagree. The grasshopper wants to spend the fall relaxing outside, while the ant wants to prepare for winter. In your opinion, who made the smarter choice, the grasshopper or the ant?

After you figure out what you need to answer, review important details from the text to develop your ideas.

Forming Your Opinion

So, what do you think? Was the grasshopper right to spend the fall relaxing, or was the ant right to spend the fall preparing for winter? Your answer to that question is your **opinion**. Here's one student's opinion.

> The ant was right: preparing for winter was the smarter choice.

Listing Your Reasons

If you want your opinion to be convincing, you need to support it with **reasons**. Your reasons should be based on details from the text. List your reasons before you write.

My Opinion	Reasons for My Opinion
The ant was right: preparing for winter was the smarter choice.	1. When winter came, the ant had plenty of food because she spent the fall gathering grain from the field. 2. The grasshopper almost starved because he didn't prepare for winter.

To further support your opinion, think of ways you could defend it against a different opinion. For example, someone else may say that the grasshopper made the smarter choice because he got to enjoy the nice fall weather before having to stay inside all winter. You can contrast this idea to add more support to your opinion.

> The grasshopper enjoyed the fall weather instead of gathering food. <u>Therefore</u>, he almost starved during the winter. The ant's choice was smarter <u>because</u> it kept her from starving in the winter.

Linking words and phrases such as *because*, *therefore*, and *for example* help to show how your ideas are related. Look at how these words are used above to connect ideas.

Writing a Good Conclusion

After you give all your reasons, go back to your opinion and end your essay with a strong **conclusion** that persuades readers to agree with your opinion.

> The fable "The Grasshopper and the Ant" teaches the important lesson that it is better to plan ahead. The grasshopper learned what the ant knew all along: if you don't plan for the future, you will not be prepared when the future comes.

Finishing Up

Be sure you reread your writing to check that your opinion is clear and your reasons are well organized. Proofread your work for spelling mistakes and other errors. Use this checklist to help you.

- ☐ Does my response answer all parts of the prompt?
- ☐ Do I state my opinion clearly in the first paragraph?
- ☐ Do I include enough reasons to support my opinion?
- ☐ Is my response well organized?
- ☐ Do I provide a strong conclusion?
- ☐ Is my writing free of mistakes?

Language Spotlight • Verb Tenses

A **verb** is a word that shows action. The **tense** of a verb shows when the action happened—in the past, the present, or the future.

Past Tense	Present Tense	Future Tense
Ava walked to school.	Ava walks to school.	Ava will walk to school.
Dad cooked dinner.	Dad cooks dinner.	Dad will cook dinner.

When you write, use the same **verb tense** throughout. The exception to this rule relates to writing dialogue. Dialogue in a story may be written in the present tense even though actions in the story are written in the past tense. For example, look at the words *want* and *wanted* in the example below.

Lee wanted a sandwich. "I want a sandwich," Lee said.

Complete these sentences using the correct form of the verb *watch*.

"Let's _____ the baseball game," Pedro said.

The boys _____ the game together.

Read the passage.

Donkey and Friends Find a New Home

adapted from a folktale by the Grimm Brothers

A farmer had an old donkey that was no longer of use, so the farmer decided to get rid of it. The donkey knew what was about to happen and ran away.

As the donkey walked along the road, it came upon a dog. The dog was lying on the ground and panting.

"Hello, Dog," said Donkey. "Is something wrong?"

"My owner was going to give me away because I am old and no longer able to hunt. So I ran away," said the dog.

The two animals became friends and continued down the road together. Soon, they saw a cat with a very sad face.

"Hello, Cat," said Donkey. "Is something wrong?"

"My owner threatened to drown me because I am old and I nap by the fire instead of catching mice. So I ran away."

"Come with us," said Donkey. The cat was happy to join them. The three animals came to a farm. A rooster was crowing as if its life depended on it.

"Hello, Rooster," said Donkey. "Is something wrong?"

"The farmer's wife wants to put me in a soup!" the rooster crowed.

"Come with us," said Donkey. So the rooster joined the party.

The sun began to set, and the animals looked for a place to sleep. Rooster flew up to the top of a tree. He saw a light nearby. "I see a house," he called to his friends.

"Let's find it," Donkey suggested. "Maybe there's a yard where we can sleep safely."

The animals found the house, and Donkey peeked in through a window. He saw robbers sitting around a table, counting their money. The house looked like a comfortable place to sleep, but first they had to get rid of the robbers.

"I have a plan," said Donkey. He shared his idea with his friends, and they agreed to work together. Donkey put his front legs up on the window ledge. Dog climbed onto his back. Then, Cat climbed onto Dog's shoulders. Finally, Rooster flew up and sat on Cat's head.

When the robbers turned to the window, they thought they saw a horrible monster. Then, the animals all made as much noise as they could. Donkey brayed, Dog barked, Cat meowed, and Rooster crowed. The robbers fled in fear, never to return. The animals were so pleased with their new home that they never left.

Answer the following questions.

1 This question has two parts. First, answer Part A. Then, answer Part B.

Part A

Two students wrote the following opinions about "Donkey and Friends Find a New Home." Circle the opinion that is **best** supported by evidence in the story.

Opinion 1	The animals are able to get a new home because they work together.
Opinion 2	Donkey would have found a better home if he were by himself.
Opinion 3	The animals are happy with their new home because they can live in it together.

Part B

Underline a sentence in the story that supports your answer to Part A.

Hint Reread the part of the story in which the animals find their new home. How are they able to scare the robbers away?

2 Each choice on the left is missing a word or phrase. Complete each choice by matching it to the correct linking word or phrase on the right.

A. In many ways, Donkey acts as a leader. _____, he comes up with the plan for how to take over the house.

1. Therefore

B. The animals are desperate to find a solution _____ they know their owners want them gone.

2. For example

C. Donkey has the best ideas. _____, the other animals listen to him.

3. because

Hint Think about how you would use each linking word or phrase. Which one makes sense in each sentence?

3 What do you think the author is trying to show about Donkey's character by having him come up with a plan to scare away the robbers?

A. Donkey is easily frightened.

B. Donkey is a brave leader.

C. Donkey only looks out for himself.

D. Donkey is used to scaring robbers.

Hint Think about how Donkey acts throughout the story. Which statement makes sense with what you already know about his character?

4 In this story, Donkey has two problems, one that happens near the beginning of the story and one that happens near the end. On the lines below, explain what each problem is and how he solves it.

_____

_____

_____

_____

_____

_____

_____

_____

_____

_____

_____

Hint Think about why Donkey doesn't have a home in the beginning of the story. Then, think about what stands in his way once he finds a new home.

Use the Reading Guide to help you understand the passage.

Fishling and Friends and Big Green Eel

Reading Guide

How does the author show Fishling's character in this part of the story?

Why are the animals left without a home?

In what ways are Fishling, Crawlette, and Sea-Kitten like the animals in "Donkey and Friends Find a New Home"?

How does the author show Sea-Kitten's feelings about scaring away Big Green Eel?

Fishling liked to swim near the opening of the underwater cave where he lived with Crawlette and Sea-Kitten. Sometimes a big jacklefish swam by. Then, Fishling would duck into the cave. He felt safe there. Crawlette liked to scurry along the floor of the cave. She found tasty things to eat and rarely left the cozy cave. Sea-Kitten liked to nap on the soft seaweed on the side of the cave. The three small sea creatures were happy in their cave until the day Big Green Eel moved in.

Big Green Eel was known to steal the homes of smaller sea creatures. He slipped past Fishling and swam right into the cave. Water rushed out of the cave with a WHOOSH, taking Sea-Kitten and Crawlette with it. They ended up floating next to Fishling.

"What are we going to do?" asked Sea-Kitten. "Where can we live now?"

"Let's crawl back inside when Big Green Eel isn't looking," said Crawlette. "He might not even notice us."

"I don't think so," said Fishling. "The cave isn't big enough for all of us. Besides, I don't trust Big Green Eel. He might eat us!" Fishling's fins shuddered at the thought of becoming Big Green Eel's next meal. "I have a better idea. Let's scare him away!"

"That's a great idea!" said Crawlette.

But Sea-Kitten was not so sure. "How can three little sea creatures like us scare away Big Green Eel? We're the ones who are scared!"

Reading Guide

What message do you think the author is trying to give about working together?

What details does the author include to show how the animals make Big Green Eel go away?

What details does the author include to show Fishling's leadership skills?

Fishling swam in a circle, thinking.

"I know!" he cried. "We have to fool Big Green Eel into thinking that an even bigger and scarier animal is living in the cave. Then, he will leave our cave and never come back."

"That's a great idea!" said Crawlette. And Sea-Kitten agreed.

When Big Green Eel left the cave to hunt, the three little sea creatures snuck back into the cave. They brought along two small shells filled with glow-worms. They placed the shells with the glowing worms at the back of the cave, far enough apart so they looked like the eyes of a big, scary animal. Then, they waited.

Finally, Big Green Eel came back to the cave to sleep. He saw two eyes glowing in the back of the cave. Curious, he went farther in. The three brave sea creatures sprang into action. Sea-Kitten scratched Big Green Eel's nose. Crawlette flipped her tail in Big Green Eel's eye. Fishling used his fins to push water along Big Green Eel's body, as if a much bigger sea creature were swimming right next to him.

Half-blinded and annoyed, Big Green Eel cried out, "I'm being attacked by a huge sea monster!" He swam out of the cave and never returned.

Answer the following questions.

1 This question has two parts. First, answer Part A. Then, answer Part B.

Part A

Which statement about Fishling is supported by evidence in the story?

A. Fishling is determined to get his home back.

B. Fishling is more fearful than Sea-Kitten.

C. Fishling needs a bigger home.

D. Fishling is not as smart as Big Green Eel.

Part B

Write a detail from the story that supports your answer to Part A.

_____

_____

2 Read these sentences from the story.

> **Sea-Kitten scratched Big Green Eel's nose. Crawlette flipped her tail in Big Green Eel's eye. Fishling used his fins to push water along Big Green Eel's body, as if a much bigger sea creature were swimming right next to him.**

These sentences tell what each animal does to scare away Big Green Eel. Why do you think the author includes these details? Circle **all** that apply.

A. to show that the animals are working together

B. to show that Big Green Eel is easy to scare

C. to show that Sea-Kitten is still scared of Big Green Eel

D. to show how the animals trick Big Green Eel into thinking they are a big sea monster

E. to show how each character behaves bravely

3 A student wrote the following opinion about Sea-Kitten.

> **Sea-Kitten is fearful at first, but she gains courage as the story goes on.**

Underline a sentence or sentences from the story that the student could use as reasons to support her opinion.

4 Write an opinion about Big Green Eel's actions. Use details from the text to support your opinion. Include a linking word or phrase to connect your opinion and reason.

_____

_____

_____

_____

5 A student wrote the following paragraph about "Fishling and Friends and Big Green Eel."

> **The animals should not have attacked Big Green Eel because it's possible that Big Green Eel didn't mean to steal their home. The animals don't know why Big Green Eel moved in because they don't try to talk to him before forcing him out.**

Which of these is the **best** concluding statement for this paragraph?

A. Big Green Eel was a terrible monster that needed to be defeated.

B. Sea-Kitten, Fishling, and Crawlette were right to take what was theirs.

C. The animals should have talked to Big Green Eel before deciding what to do.

D. Talking to Big Green Eel would not have changed the fact that he was greedy.

6 You have read about two strong main characters, Fishling and Donkey, who lead their friends to scare away an enemy. Write a response that gives your opinion about whose actions took more bravery, Fishling's or Donkey's.

Be sure to support your writing with examples from both stories and include a concluding statement in your response.

You may plan your writing in the space below. Then, write your response on the following pages.

Plan

Write your response on the lines below.

Write a Story

As a reader, you can enjoy different types of stories. Authors write stories to entertain readers. Thinking about how authors create interesting stories can help you write your own stories.

All stories have characters, a setting, a plot, and a point of view. Think about a new story you might like to write. Ask yourself questions to help you brainstorm. What kind of characters would you like to write about? Do you want your story to take place in the past, present, or future? Who should tell your story? What will happen in your story? Will the story be funny, exciting, or even sad?

Planning Your Story

Choose a setting, characters, plot, and point of view

- Choose a **setting** based on what kind of story you want to tell. For example, if you're writing a fantasy story, you might set it in an imaginary world.

- The **characters** perform the action in your narrative. Think about what you want your characters to be like and how you want their actions to affect the sequence of events.

- To plan the **plot**, think about what will happen in the beginning, middle, and end of the story. What conflict, or problem, will the characters have to solve?

- Choose a **point of view**. Will the story be told by one of the characters or by a narrator outside of the story?

Organize the plot Suppose you are writing a story about a caterpillar who wants to turn into a chicken instead of a butterfly. The characters will be a caterpillar, a butterfly, and a chicken, and the setting will be a farm. You might plan out your plot using a flowchart like the one on the next page.

Beginning	Middle	End
Conflict: Caterpillar loves the farm where she grew up. She doesn't want to become a butterfly and have to fly away from home.	**Event 1:** Caterpillar talks to a chicken at the farm who says caterpillars never grow into chickens, only into butterflies. **Event 2:** Caterpillar talks to a wise, old butterfly who explains that Caterpillar will become a butterfly and fly away, but then she can come back.	**Resolution:** Caterpillar becomes a butterfly and flies south. After her long journey, she returns to the farm and lays her eggs.

Writing Your First Draft

How a story is organized has a big effect on how well readers understand and enjoy it. These storytelling tips can help you write an organized draft.

Establish a situation In the beginning, introduce when and where the story takes place, who the characters are, and what it is about.

- Some stories start right in the middle of the action. Others grab readers' attention with an interesting description of the setting or one of the characters.

- Introduce the conflict early. This gives your readers a reason to keep reading: to find out how the conflict will be resolved!

Organize the events When you write a story, be sure that your readers can follow the **sequence** of events so they know what happens first, next, and last.

- **Time-order words** can help make the sequence of events clear. Words like *first, then, next, immediately, soon,* and *later* tell when the events are happening and how much time passes between them.

- Make sure each event follows the next in a natural way. The events should lead to a satisfying ending that shows how the characters solve the problem.

Add description and dialogue Without description and dialogue, a story is just a summary. A good **description** helps readers picture the characters and events in their minds. When you *show* the events and let characters speak through **dialogue**, your readers feel like they are part of the story. Describing the characters' actions, thoughts, and feelings brings their experiences to life and helps your readers relate to them.

Revising and Editing Your Story

Remember to reread your story and make revisions before handing it in. When you revise, put yourself in your reader's shoes. Would a reader be able to follow your story? Would he or she find it interesting? Ask yourself:

- ☐ Does the beginning establish a situation with a setting, characters, plot conflict, and point of view?

- ☐ Is the sequence of events clear?

- ☐ Do I develop the characters in an interesting way?

- ☐ Do I use dialogue and description?

- ☐ Does my ending follow from the events in the story?

Also make sure to edit your story. Check for and fix any mistakes in spelling or grammar.

Language Spotlight • Quotation Marks and Commas

When you write dialogue, remember to use the correct **punctuation**. Use quotation marks at the beginning and end of the words a character says. Use a comma to separate the character's words from his or her name. Circle the quotation marks and comma in the sentence below.

"I want to stay at the farm," Caterpillar said.

Read the passage.

The Weather Machine

"Do you want to play a board game, Grandma?" asked Owen as he walked into the small workroom on the side of the garage. It was a rainy day, and Owen was bored.

Grandma was holding an old clock radio in one hand. Her other hand was reaching for her favorite screwdriver.

"Not right now, dear. Can you find my reading glasses for me?" she asked. Grandma always forgot where she put her glasses. This time they were resting on top of her forehead.

"They're on your head," said Owen. Grandma had her hands full, so he gently pushed them down over her eyes for her.

"Thank you, dear. Now I can see what I'm doing." Grandma tinkered some more with the clock radio.

"Are you fixing that for Dad?" Owen asked. The back of the clock radio had been removed. The multicolored wires were all tangled up.

"No, your father said he doesn't need it now that he has a cool new phone with all the latest features. I decided to use the radio for something else," Grandma said without looking up from her work.

A bolt of lightning streaked across the sky outside the window, immediately followed by a boom of thunder. Owen remembered something.

"Hey, wasn't your picnic supposed to be today?" he asked. Once a year Grandma and her cousins had a fancy picnic in the park. Owen knew that Grandma had been looking forward to that special occasion all month.

"It was canceled due to rain," she said. "I'm sick and tired of the weather controlling me, so I decided to control the weather."

Grandma put the back of the clock radio in place. "There! I'm done!" She turned a dial and pushed a button. Immediately, the rain that had been falling all day stopped.

"Did you do that?" Owen asked, amazed that anyone might be able to control the weather.

"I didn't," Grandma said modestly, "but my new weather machine did."

Grandma's weather machine worked so well that people all over town asked to borrow it for picnics, ball games, parades, and even weddings. It got to the point where Owen's neighborhood hadn't had a drop of rain for over two months. Then, Owen saw in the news that a local farmer complained that his crops were dying from lack of rain. Owen wondered if maybe Grandma's weather machine was giving them too much of a good thing.

Answer the following questions.

1 Read the paragraph from the story below.

> **"Do you want to play a board game, Grandma?" asked Owen as he walked into the small workroom on the side of the garage. It was a rainy day, and Owen was bored.**

Underline the words that the author uses to introduce the setting.

Hint Remember that the setting is where and when the story takes place.

2 Find a sentence on page 184 in which the author includes a time-order word or phrase to make the sequence of events clear. Copy the sentence below, and underline the time-order word or phrase.

_____

_____

_____

_____

> **Hint** Remember that a time-order words gives a clue about the order of events. It tells when things happen or in what order.

3 Which line of dialogue does the author include in the story to show how Grandma responds to her picnic being canceled?

A. "Not right now, dear. Can you find my reading glasses for me?"

B. "Thank you, dear. Now I can see what I'm doing."

C. "I'm sick and tired of the weather controlling me, so I decided to control the weather."

D. "There! I'm done!"

> **Hint** Think about what Grandma does as a result of her picnic being canceled. How does she explain it to Owen?

4 "The Weather Machine" ends with farmers complaining that there is not enough rain to grow crops. What else might happen because of Grandma's weather machine? Write an original story to continue "The Weather Machine" and provide a satisfying ending. Your story should include dialogue, description, and time-order words.

_____

_____

_____

_____

_____

_____

_____

_____

_____

_____

_____

_____

_____

_____

_____

Hint The end of the story introduces a problem caused by the weather machine. How can your story solve that problem?

Use the Reading Guide to help you understand the passage.

A Tale of Two Pirates

Reading Guide

Where does the author introduce the setting?

What does the dialogue in this section show about Pirate Gnastie's character?

Which parts of the story make it funny?

A poor fishing village had finally saved enough silver coins to build its first school. The people were celebrating when a pirate ship sailed ashore.

"Give me your silver or I will burn down your village," a pirate threatened.

"Who is he?" asked one child.

"He's a nasty pirate," whispered his mother.

"I heard that!" said the pirate. "So you *have* heard of me! Yes, my name is Gnastie! The 'G' is silent," he explained to the puzzled villagers.

Pirate Gnastie's mates took all the silver coins.

"But we were going to use that silver to build our school," said the child.

"Hush!" warned his mother.

But Pirate Gnastie seemed pleased by the child's remark. "Building a school is a waste of good silver. I never went to school, and look at how well I turned out!"

His statement was met with silence and odd looks. The villagers did not think he had turned out so well at all.

"There hasn't been a school in this part of the world for as long as I've been alive, and there's no reason to build one now that I'm too old to go," he added spitefully. "If I didn't get to go to school, no one will!"

Pirate Gnastie had finished his speech. His mates loaded the stolen silver onto the ship. Now it was time to leave.

"Good-bye!" said Pirate Gnastie.

Reading Guide

How does the author show time passing in this part of the story?

Why do the characters send a message out to sea?

What does Captain Givesback's dialogue reveal about his character?

The child watched the pirate ship sail away. "Who can help us now?" he asked sadly.

"Captain Givesback!" the villagers said together. The mayor of the village agreed with their idea. He wrote a plea for help on a piece of paper. He put their message inside a bottle, plugged up the bottle, and tossed it into the sea.

"Who's Captain Givesback?" asked the child. He was too young to remember the last time this kind, brave pirate had helped the villagers.

"Captain Givesback is a good pirate. He finds treasure that bad pirates have stolen and returns it to their rightful owners," explained the child's father. "He will get our silver back so you and the other children can have your school."

And sure enough, before sunset, Captain Givesback had sailed ashore.

The villagers crowded around him. "Can you help us?" asked the child.

"I will try my best," said Givesback. "But I happen to know that Gnastie is very bitter about not getting to go to school. As nasty as he is, sometimes I feel bad for him. But stealing coins is unacceptable! I will follow him to the end of the ocean if I must!"

Just then, a pigeon landed on the good pirate's shoulder. Captain Givesback took the small scroll of paper the bird held in its beak and read it quickly.

"I must be off at once," he said. "Gnastie has been spotted in Baytown with the coins! Set sail for Baytown!"

Captain Givesback and his mates sailed off, rowing with all their might. They found Pirate Gnastie dragging a heavy bag of coins to the Baytown Bank.

"You there!" Captain Givesback cried. "Stop at once!"

Answer the following questions.

1 Read this paragraph from the story.

> **"I will try my best," said Givesback. "But I happen to know that Gnastie is very bitter about not getting to go to school. As nasty as he is, sometimes I feel bad for him. But stealing coins is unacceptable! I will follow him to the end of the ocean if I must!"**

What does the author show about Captain Givesback's character by including these lines of dialogue?

A. Captain Givesback is sure he can catch Pirate Gnastie but wants Gnastie to go to school first.

B. Captain Givesback feels sorry for Pirate Gnastie, but he also believes in doing the right thing.

C. Captain Givesback has gotten lazy about chasing bad pirates, and he will probably give up on getting the silver back.

D. Captain Givesback thinks Pirate Gnastie is the worst person he has ever met and doesn't feel sorry for him.

2 Captain Givesback responds quickly to the villagers' plea for help. Underline the sentence from the story that uses time-order words to make this fact clear.

3 The following question has two parts. First, answer Part A. Then, answer Part B.

Part A

On the lines below, explain how the author introduces the story's conflict.

_____

_____

Part B

Which sentence from the story shows how the villagers respond to the conflict?

A. The people were celebrating when a pirate ship sailed ashore.

B. Pirate Gnastie's mates took all the silver coins.

C. He wrote a plea for help on a piece of paper.

D. Just then, a pigeon landed on the good pirate's shoulder.

4 Write numbers 1 through 5 in the boxes below to show how the author organizes the sequence of events in this story.

☐ The villagers save enough silver to build a school.

☐ Captain Givesback finds Pirate Gnastie.

☐ Pirate Gnastie steals the villagers' silver.

☐ Captain Givesback arrives in the fishing village.

☐ The villagers write to Captain Givesback for help.

5 Write **two** sentences from the story, either dialogue or description, that show Pirate Gnastie's character.

_____

_____

_____

6 The story ends with Captain Givesback tracking down Pirate Gnastie. Think about the details the author used to describe both characters. Then, write an original story to continue "A Tale of Two Pirates." Use what you have learned about the main characters to tell what they do next and how the story ends.

Be sure to:

- organize an event sequence that unfolds naturally.

- use time-order words and phrases to make the sequence of events clear.

- include dialogue and description to bring the events to life.

- write an ending that resolves the conflict.

You may plan your story in the space below. Then, write your response on the following pages.

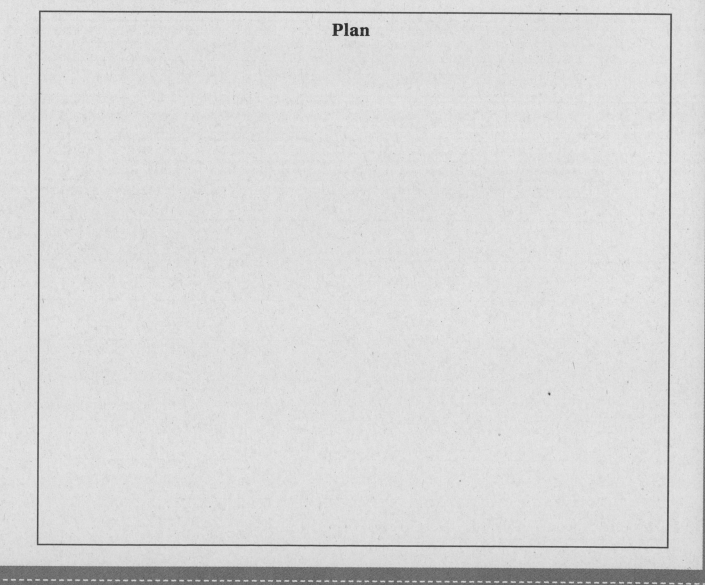

Plan

Write your story on the lines below.

W.3.6, W.3.7, W.3.8, L.3.2.a

Research Skills

1 GETTING THE IDEA

Sometimes, you are asked to write a **report**, or informational article, about things that you do not know a lot about. When this happens, you need to do some **research** first. Doing research means that you gather facts and information from different sources. You do research to learn more about a **topic**. Then, you use what you learned to write about it.

Suppose your teacher gave you the following report topic: *How do police officers help to keep us safe?*

Here are the steps you would take to research this topic.

Recall Information

First, recall information from your own personal experiences with police officers. Write a short description of these experiences, and explain how the officers kept you or others safe. These notes will help you later when you write your report.

Get Information

Next, get some additional information from other sources. A **source** is any material that helps a writer find information. There are two main places you can do a basic search for information: the library and the Internet.

- The **library** is filled with books, magazines, encyclopedias, and many other sources on various topics. It is a great place to start your research.

- The **Internet** is very helpful. You must be careful, though. Some Web sites have correct facts, but others do not. Find two or more sources that agree. Then you know you have facts you can trust!

The list below describes the types of sources you can use.

Encyclopedias: Have facts that can be trusted; are a good starting point for research; do not give a lot of detail about a topic. Example: an encyclopedia entry for "Police Departments"

Nonfiction books: Have many facts and details that have been checked and can be trusted. Example: *All About Our Police Force*

Magazines and newspapers: Have facts and details that can be trusted; may give opinions about different topics. Examples: *Police Digest; The Daily Police Bulletin*

Web sites: Have many facts that are easily available; usually give current information. Examples: Web sites ending in .gov, .edu, and .org

Remember that your sources should always relate to your topic. When finding sources, look through each one or read its table of contents to make sure it has the information you need.

It is also very important to use trustworthy resources. These are sources that have correct facts and details. Be especially careful with Web sites. Make sure you use a site you can trust, such as ones ending in .gov, .edu, and .org. You do not want to write a report based on opinions, incomplete facts, or information that is not correct.

Gather Information

Once you have your sources, your next step is to take notes from them. This involves writing down important facts, details, numbers, and quotes from each source. When taking notes, gather only the information that you think you'll use when you write your report. Do not take notes on any other information.Use index cards to write down each fact or detail from a source. Remember to record the name of the source, the author of the source, and the page on which you found the information. You will use this information to create a bibliography. A **bibliography** lists each source you used to write your report.

Sort Information

Sort your information by creating categories. The chart shows how one student sorted information about police officers.

How Police Keep Us Safe

Fighting Crime	Making Sure We Follow the Rules	Helping Us Solve Problems
putting criminals in jail	handing out speeding tickets	helping kids and other people who are lost
stopping crimes before they happen	responding to neighborhood complaints	helping us in an emergency

There are many different ways to sort information. You can use a chart like this one or another kind of graphic organizer. The important thing is to make sure you put your facts and details into categories so that you can figure out how to plan your writing.

Once you have finished organizing your notes, the only thing left to do is write your report!

Language Spotlight • Capitalization in Titles

When you create a bibliography for your report, you will need to list the titles of sources. Here are some guidelines to follow for capitalizing titles.

- Capitalize the first and last words in the title and all nouns, pronouns, adjectives, verbs, and adverbs.

- Do *not* capitalize articles, conjunctions, and prepositions.

Look at the examples below. Then, use the guidelines to correctly write the title of a book you read recently.

Bunnicula   "How to Build a Birdhouse"

Read the passage from an online encyclopedia.

Police Horses

Police horses help **police officers** do their jobs. The officers ride the horses while on patrol. Police horses help officers:
- see a large area and quickly identify problems.
- get into areas that a car or bicycle cannot.
- hold back or control large crowds of people.
- monitor events such as parades or festivals.

A police officer must be able to trust his or her horse. **Police departments** look for horses that are large, gentle, and easy to train. A police horse must be able to stay calm in an emergency. It must not run away. This could put the officer in danger.

Evaluation

Horses are evaluated, or tested, to see if they would do well on the **police force**. The evaluation period usually lasts two or three months. Horses must walk through smoke. They must stand near loud fireworks. They are introduced to loud crowds of people. They may be brought to a busy city street to see how they will react. Horses are also tested to see how they get along with officers and other horses.

A good police horse will:
- be calm and gentle.
- be in good physical shape.
- get along with people and other horses.
- not be frightened by loud noises and large crowds.

Training

About one horse out of every five will pass the evaluation period. It will then move on to training. It will learn to be a police horse during this period. Trainers introduce the horse to new situations. It will learn to walk through crowds of people. It will learn to stand still for long periods of time. It will learn to always obey its officer's commands. Trainers teach the horse not to be afraid or run away.

When a horse has completed its training, it is paired with a police officer who will ride it. The horse and the officer are now partners. Together, they work to keep their community safe.

Answer the following questions.

1 Peter is doing research for a report on types of horses that are good for police work. Read the paragraphs from "Police Horses." Then, follow the directions below.

> **Police horses help police officers do their jobs. The officers ride the horses while on patrol. Police horses help officers:**
> - **see a large area and quickly identify problems.**
> - **get into areas that a car or bicycle cannot.**
> - **hold back or control large crowds of people.**
> - **monitor events such as parades or festivals.**
>
> **A police officer must be able to trust his or her horse. Police departments look for horses that are large, gentle, and easy to train. A police horse must be able to stay calm in an emergency. It must not run away. This could put the officer in danger.**

Underline the information in the paragraphs that Peter can use in his report about good police horses.

Hint Search the passage for key words that describe good police horses. What are these horses like? What do they do?

2 Emmy is writing a report about how police horses are chosen. She is sorting evidence from "Police Horses." Look at the chart. Then, answer Part A and Part B below.

Evaluation	walk through smoke
	stand near fireworks
	meet other officers and horses
Training	
	walk through crowds
	obey officer's commands
	stay calm instead of running away

Part A

Which evidence belongs in the section "Evaluation" in Emmy's chart?

A. have a police officer as a partner

B. are brought to a busy street

C. walk away from a loud crowd

D. keep the community safe

Part B

Which evidence belongs in the section "Training" in Emmy's chart?

Write your answer on the lines below.

_____

_____

Hint Look for headings in the passage to help you know where the details belong in the chart. Remember to check your answer against the information in "Police Horses." In addition, be sure to go back and reread the section "Training."

3 Gabe is doing research for a report about how police horses help officers. Read his notes from "Police Horses." Then, answer Part A and Part B below.

Notes
• Police horses get into areas where cars and bicycles cannot go.
• Police horses must be easy to train.
• A police officer must be able to trust his or her horse.
• Police horses always obey their officers' commands.
• A police officer uses a police horse to keep a community safe.

Part A

Cross out any notes in Gabe's research that do not belong.

Part B

Explain why the notes you crossed out in Part A do not belong in Gabe's research.

_____

_____

_____

_____

> **Hint** Reread the beginning of the question. What is the topic of Gabe's report? Look for notes that do not directly relate to this topic.

4 Marta is writing a report on how other animals help the police. What is the best source for Marta to use to begin her research?

A. a Web site for the local police department in Marta's town

B. a magazine article describing ways that dogs can help communities

C. an encyclopedia article that explains how a police department works

D. a nonfiction book about how police use dogs to find missing people

Hint Remember that Marta's report is about animals and how they help police. Which source relates to both an animal and the police?

Use the Reading Guide to help you understand the passage.

A Day in the Life of a Police Horse

by Daniel Garza

Reading Guide

What is the author's purpose for writing this passage? How do you know?

How does Walter feel about Charlie? Why do you think he feels that way?

Look at the details under "7:15 a.m." Which details would be helpful for a research report about police horses?

It is early morning on a cool September day at River Stables. The sun is just beginning to rise as Walter Everson brings Charlie out to meet me. Charlie is a police horse. He has been with the Riverside Police Department for six years. Walter tells me that Charlie is the best partner he has ever had. That is saying a lot. Walter has been a police officer for twenty-five years. He has had a few partners—human *and* horse.

The best thing about my job as a newspaper reporter is the great people I meet and interview. I feel lucky to get to spend a day with this pair!

6:30 a.m.

I finish my coffee as Walter brushes Charlie and puts on the riding equipment. Charlie snorts loudly. He is ready to go! I hop in the truck while Walter puts Charlie in the trailer. Walter gets in the driver's seat, and we head to Riverside City Park to start our day.

7:15 a.m.

Walter parks the trailer and leads Charlie out. Now Walter and Charlie are on patrol as I walk beside them. Walter is high up on Charlie and can see all around him. He looks for signs of trouble at the park.

"I have been a mounted police officer for ten years, and I love it," says Walter. "Charlie and I have searched through woods for missing people. We have made arrests together and given out tickets. We have even held back crowds at parades. I can always count on Charlie to help me."

Keep an eye out for factual details and evidence that supports them.

How does Charlie act during rush hour? How does he help Walter during the accident? What does Charlie do in front of City Hall? Think about how Charlie's actions help Walter do his job.

8:15 a.m.

We finish our tour of the park and head into the city. It is rush hour and very noisy. Cars are beeping. There is also a construction project down the street. Charlie just looks around and snorts. He doesn't mind at all.

8:25 a.m.

Some kids run up to us. They ask if they can pet Charlie. Walter says, "Yes, of course!" I get the feeling that it happens all the time. The parents ask for directions to a local museum, and Walter points the way.

9:10 a.m.

Suddenly, there is a loud crunching noise down the block. It looks like a car accident. Walter urges Charlie into a trot, and they move down the street ahead of me.

9:20 a.m.

Walter takes notes for an accident report. Thankfully, no one is hurt. The drivers are fighting, though. Walter moves Charlie between the two angry men to separate them as he finishes taking notes.

11:00 a.m.

We head back to the trailer for lunch. Walter removes Charlie's bridle and ties him to the trailer. Charlie stands and waits for his partner to give him hay and water. Then, Walter and I sit down to eat our lunch.

11:50 a.m.

Walter gets a call on his radio. He and Charlie must meet up with other officers. They are outside City Hall, where people are gathering with signs. They are protesting a new law. The officers will make sure no one gets hurt.

Reading Guide

Remember that a good research report is supported by evidence. What evidence shows that Charlie can control a crowd?

12:10 p.m.

We arrive at City Hall and find a large crowd. Walter asks me to stay back. He moves Charlie into the crowd. I watch as people back away. Charlie does the work of many police officers on foot. He is able to calmly control the situation.

2:30 p.m.

Walter puts Charlie back into the trailer. Finally we all head back to River Stables. It has been a long day, but Charlie does not look tired at all. He really loves his job!

Walter grooms Charlie and lets him out in a fenced paddock. A stable worker will bring him in later and give him dinner. "See you tomorrow, buddy!" Walter shouts as we leave. Charlie snorts in reply. I have a feeling he is looking forward to it!

Answer the following questions.

1 Keira is doing research for a report about police horses in the city where she lives. Her teacher has asked her to include information from any personal experiences she might have had.

Which would be the **best** example of a personal experience that Keira could use in her report?

A. describing the day she saw police on horses during a parade and telling what they did

B. telling about the time a police officer visited her school to talk about safety rules

C. telling about her cousin's pony and how it looks a lot like a police horse

D. describing the first time she rode a horse and how it felt to sit in the saddle

2 Miguel is sorting details from "A Day in the Life of a Police Horse." Look at the diagram that Miguel created. Then, read the directions below.

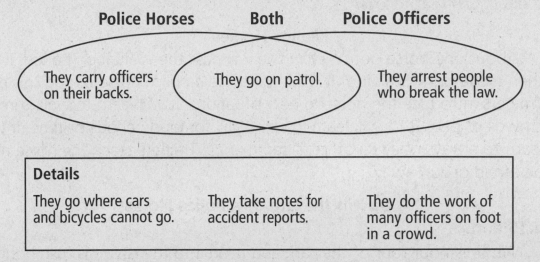

Police Horses   **Both**   **Police Officers**

They carry officers on their backs.   They go on patrol.   They arrest people who break the law.

Details

They go where cars and bicycles cannot go.   They take notes for accident reports.   They do the work of many officers on foot in a crowd.

Help Miguel finish sorting the information from the passage. Draw arrows from each detail in the box to show where it belongs in the diagram.

3 Kate is writing a research report about how police horses are trained. Read the paragraphs from the two sources that you have already reviewed. Then, read the directions that follow.

"Police Horses"

About one horse out of every five will pass the evaluation period. It will then move on to training. It will learn to be a police horse during this period. Trainers introduce the horse to new situations. It will learn to walk through crowds of people. It will learn to stand still for long periods of time. It will learn to always obey its officer's commands. Trainers teach the horse not to be afraid or run away.

"A Day in the Life of a Police Horse"

8:15 a.m.

We finish our tour of the park and head into the city. It is rush hour and very noisy. Cars are beeping. There is also a construction project down the street. Charlie just looks around and snorts. He doesn't mind at all.

Choose **one** sentence from **each** source that Kate could use to show that horses are trained to be calm.

A. About one horse out of every five will pass the evaluation period.

B. It will learn to walk through crowds of people.

C. Trainers teach the horse not to be afraid or run away.

D. It is rush hour and very noisy.

E. There is also a construction project down the street.

F. He doesn't mind at all.

4 A student is writing a report on what police horses do during the day. He is taking notes on "A Day in the Life of a Police Horse." Read the paragraphs from the passage and the directions that follow.

11:50 a.m.

Walter gets a call on his radio. He and Charlie must meet up with other officers. They are outside City Hall, where people are gathering with signs. They are protesting a new law. The officers will make sure no one gets hurt.

12:10 p.m.

We arrive at City Hall and find a large crowd. Walter asks me to stay back. He moves Charlie into the crowd. I watch as people back away. Charlie does the work of many police officers on foot. He is able to calmly control the situation.

Use details from the passage above to complete the student's notes. Write your answers on the lines provided in the Notes box.

Notes
1. Police horses meet up with other officers.
2. Police horses _____
_____ .
3. Police horses _____
_____ .

5 The following question has two parts. First, answer Part A. Then, answer Part B.

Victor is doing research for a report on how police horses help reduce crime in the city. He is beginning his research on the Internet.

Part A

Which source should Victor look at to find facts and numbers that relate to his topic?

A. a horse magazine for riders of all ages

B. a government Web site on police officers and police horses

C. a student encyclopedia about horses

D. a nonfiction book about joining the police force

Part B

Explain why you chose this source. Write your answer on the lines below.

_____

_____

_____

_____

_____

_____

_____

_____

_____

_____

6 You have read two passages describing police horses. Both give information about what police horses do and how they help in our communities. The two passages are:

- an online encyclopedia entry titled "Police Horses."

- a newspaper article titled "A Day in the Life of a Police Horse."

Think about how each passage describes police horses. Then, think about how the passages are alike and how they are different.

Write at least three paragraphs that explain how both passages are helpful in different ways for a research report about police horses. Remember to use details from each passage to support your ideas.

You may plan your report in the space below. Then, write the paragraphs on the following pages.

Plan

Write your paragraphs on the lines below.

_____

_____

_____

_____

_____

_____

_____

_____

_____

_____

_____

_____

_____

_____

_____

_____

W.3.2.a–d, L.3.1.i

Write an Article or Report

1 GETTING THE IDEA

An **article** or a **report** gives readers information. It tells them things they may not know. It focuses on one topic and one main idea.

In school, you may write articles and reports for different reasons. For example, you may write an article about an event for the school newspaper. Or you may write a report on mammals for science class. A how-to guide for an art project would also be a report. Your writing should always fit your task, or what you have been asked to do.

Introduce the Topic

You should start a report by introducing your topic. Use a **topic sentence** to state your main idea. Make sure your topic sentence is clear. Readers should be able to tell what the report is about.

Here is an example of a strong topic sentence.

> Chimpanzees can form close bonds with their family members.

Find the Facts

Choose **facts** and details to support your main idea. Any fact or detail you include in a report should directly relate to the topic.

Look at the details below. Which one best relates to the topic sentence above?

- Chimpanzee mothers take good care of their babies.
- Some chimps have learned to "talk" using sign language.
- Chimps often use sticks and other tools to find food.

Plan Your Report

You have written a topic sentence and collected facts and details. Now you should plan your report.

Group related ideas together. Then, place the grouped ideas in an order that makes sense. This will help readers follow the ideas and better understand what you write. A graphic organizer, such as a flowchart, can help you plan.

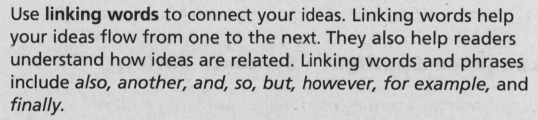

Beginning
Introduce the topic:
Chimpanzees can form close bonds with their family members.

Middle
Group ideas in order:
- Chimp mothers take good care of their babies.
- Young chimps stay with their mothers until age seven.
- Pairs of chimps often travel together.
- Chimps hoot to "call" to each other across long distances.

End
Provide a closing statement:
Having close ties with family helps young chimps as they develop and grow into young adults.

Use **linking words** to connect your ideas. Linking words help your ideas flow from one to the next. They also help readers understand how ideas are related. Linking words and phrases include *also, another, and, so, but, however, for example,* and *finally.*

Add pictures and other visuals to your report. Pictures can add information about the topic. They can also show things that might be hard to explain in words.

For example, you may want to use a photograph or an illustration to show what something looks like. Or you may want to include a diagram to show how the parts of an object work together. Any images you include should relate to the topic.

When you add an image, include labels or a caption. **Labels** name the parts in a diagram. A **caption** is the brief text below a picture or other visual that tells what it is. A caption can also explain how a visual relates to the text.

Provide a Conclusion

Be sure to wrap up your ideas at the end of a report. Use a **conclusion** to restate your topic and main ideas. You should also leave readers with a final thought about the topic. Depending on how long your piece is, your conclusion will be a single statement or a paragraph long.

Review Your Work

After you have finished, reread your writing. Make sure it is clear and easy to follow. Use this checklist as a guide.

- ☐ Is my topic sentence clear?
- ☐ Do all the facts relate to my topic?
- ☐ Do I group related ideas in a way that makes sense?
- ☐ Do I use linking words to connect my ideas?
- ☐ Do the images I used support the topic?
- ☐ Does my conclusion sum up the topic?
- ☐ Is my writing free of errors in grammar and spelling?

Language Spotlight • Sentence Variety

Use a variety of sentences to make your writing more interesting.

- A **simple sentence** has a subject and a verb. It tells a complete thought.
- A **compound sentence** is made up of two simple sentences joined by a comma and a conjunction, such as *and* or *but*.
- A **complex sentence** is made up of an incomplete thought and a complete thought joined by a conjunction, such as *if* or *when*.

Read each sentence below. Decide what kind of sentence each is.

Casey went to the library, and she worked on a report.

Casey went to the library.

After Casey went to the library, she finished the report.

Read the passage.

Animal Families

In Africa, young lion cubs play in the grass. Their mothers watch over them. If the cubs get hungry, any lioness can feed them, not just their own mother. These lions are a family, and they are called a pride. Many animals gather in family groups to survive in their environment.

Some animals like to be alone. For example, tigers tend to stay by themselves. Other animals like to live in groups. Like humans, they need close contact. So, they meet up with other animals to form communities.

Many kinds of animals live in groups. Animals of different sizes form groups. The size of the groups can also vary. For example, as many as eight to thirty wolves live in a pack. An ant colony can contain thousands of ants.

There are different reasons why animals live this way. Some animals stay in a family because it helps them find food. For example, lions often work together to hunt and kill their food. The animals that lions eat are usually faster than they are. So hunting in groups can help lions catch their prey more easily.

Forming a family can also help animals stay safe. They can keep one another warm during cold nights. They can also protect each other from predators. When a predator comes looking for food, one member of the group may warn the others. Together, the group may try to scare the predator away.

However, it is not always easy to live in an animal family. Having more members means more competition for food. Another problem is that big groups can draw more attention from predators. A whole school of fish is easier to spot than one fish swimming alone. But for many animals, living in a group is more helpful than harmful. Having family ties helps them find food and stay safe.

Animal Family Groups

Animal	Family Name
ants	colony
dolphins	pod
elephants	herd
fish	school
geese	gaggle
lions	pride
meerkats	gang, mob
rhinoceroses	crash
wolves	pack

Answer the following questions.

1 This question has two parts. First, answer Part A. Then, answer Part B.

Part A

Which sentence from the passage is the topic sentence?

A. In Africa, young lion cubs play in the grass.

B. Many animals gather in family groups to survive in their environment.

C. So, they meet up with other animals to form communities.

D. However, it is not always easy to live in an animal family.

Part B

Why is the sentence you chose in Part A an example of a strong topic sentence? Write your answer on the lines below.

_____

_____

_____

_____

_____

_____

_____

_____

_____

Hint For Part A, think about the main idea of the passage. For Part B, think about the purpose of a topic sentence.

2 Why do many animals form family groups? Write your answer on the lines below.

_____

_____

_____

_____

_____

_____

Hint Think about all the reasons the writer explains in the passage. Be sure to include any important facts in your answer.

3 Circle **two** linking words or phrases in paragraph 2 of the passage.

Hint Remember, writers use linking words to connect ideas in a text.

4 Which sentence from the passage is a compound sentence?

   A. These lions are a family, and they are called a pride.

   B. Some animals stay in a family because it helps them find food.

   C. An ant colony can contain thousands of ants.

   D. A whole school of fish is easier to spot than one fish swimming alone.

Hint A compound sentence contains two simple sentences. Each expresses a complete thought.

Use the Reading Guide to help you understand the passage.

A Community of Meerkats

Reading Guide

Find the topic sentence in paragraph 1.

Why do meerkats live in communities?

Pay attention to the details in paragraph 3. Use the information in this paragraph to describe the homes where meerkats live.

Many animals live in big groups. They come together to help one another survive. For example, fish swim in big schools, and wolves travel in large packs. Meerkats form big communities, and each community has dozens of members.

A meerkat is not a cat at all. Actually, it looks more like a weasel. It lives on the plains in the southern part of Africa. Meerkats are about the size of squirrels. They are known for standing up on their back legs. They often do this to look into the distance.

These animals gather together in big groups. Their communities are called gangs or mobs. Each one has up to forty members. Together, the animals live in homes called burrows. A burrow is a large hole under the ground. Each one has several rooms and tunnels. Living underground helps meerkats stay out of the hot African sun.

A meerkat gang can include members of different ages and sizes.

How do meerkats in a community protect one another?

How do meerkats communicate with one another?

Look at the last paragraph of the passage. What ideas does the author connect using the word *however*?

What final thought does the author leave for the reader?

Living in a big community helps these animals in different ways. For one thing, it helps them stay safe. Some birds, like eagles, hunt meerkats for food. These predators often swoop down from the sky. They can snatch a meerkat off the ground. But animals in a community can protect one another. A few meerkats serve as lookouts for the group. They keep an eye on the sky. If a bird comes close, the lookouts warn the others. They let out a sharp bark. This tells the others to find a hiding place below ground.

Meerkats also live in big communities to help one another find food. Sometimes, they work together to hunt insects, lizards, and small birds. Meerkats "talk" to each other as they hunt. They make soft, purring noises that sound like cats. Maybe that's how they got their name.

Meerkats work together in other ways. All the adults help teach the younger animals. The adults show them how to hunt for food. They show them how to hide from predators. The younger animals learn how to live in a community.

Animals that live in groups, like meerkats, are often very social. They keep one another company. They can groom each other, too. On a cold night, meerkats snuggle together to stay warm.

There are a lot of benefits to living in a community. However, there are some problems, too. It can be hard to live in such a big group. There is more competition for food. Also, it is easier for a hawk or an eagle to see a big group from high above. A meerkat living alone would be much harder to spot.

However, the benefits are worth it. Living in a community helps meerkats survive. It helps them find food and stay safe. It also helps young meerkats learn how to become adults. Without their community, life would not be the same.

Answer the following questions.

1 Look back at the photograph on page 219. How do the photograph and its caption help you better understand the information in the passage?

Write your answer on the lines below.

_____

_____

_____

_____

_____

_____

2 Read these three facts that could be added to the passage. Underline the fact that **best** relates to the topic.

Facts
Parents teach young meerkats how to spot predators.
Different kinds of weasels live all over the world.
A savannah is a flat, grassy plain found in Africa.

3 Which word does the author use to connect ideas in paragraph 8?

A. also

B. there

C. more

D. harder

4 Which sentence from the passage is a complex sentence?

A. Meerkats form big communities, and each community has dozens of members.

B. Living underground helps meerkats stay out of the hot African sun.

C. These predators often swoop down from the sky.

D. If a bird comes close, the lookouts warn the others.

5 The following question has two parts. First, answer Part A. Then, answer Part B.

Part A

How does the passage end?

A. with a topic sentence

B. with a supporting fact

C. with a concluding statement

D. with a concluding paragraph

Part B

How does the end help readers? Write your answer on the lines below.

_____

_____

_____

6 Imagine you are a scientist who has observed a meerkat community. Write a short report telling about what you observed. Include information about why many animals, including meerkats, live in groups. Be sure to give specific details about how meerkats help one another survive. Use evidence from "Animal Families" and "A Community of Meerkats" to support your response.

You may plan your report in the space below. Then, write your response on the following pages.

Plan

Write your report on the lines below.

_____

_____

_____

_____

_____

_____

_____

_____

_____

_____

_____

_____

_____

_____

_____

_____

_____

_____

Write an Opinion

❶ GETTING THE IDEA

Have you ever been asked, "What do you think?" Your response is your opinion. Your **opinion** is how you feel about something. When you write an opinion piece, you want the reader to agree with you. So, you need good, strong **reasons** that show why your opinion is correct. Use facts to support your reasons. A **fact** is information that is true and can be proved.

Remember to keep your audience in mind. Use words that fit your reader. If you write for your little sister, use easy words and short sentences. If you write for your teacher, you can use more complex words and longer sentences.

State Your Opinion

The first step in writing an opinion piece is choosing a topic. Next, decide what you think or feel about the topic. Then, use clear language to write your opinion. You want the reader to understand what you believe right from the beginning.

Here is how one third-grader introduced her topic and stated her opinion clearly.

> I think the school year should be longer so there is more time to learn.

Organize Your Information

Your opinion piece needs a beginning, middle, and end.

- In the **beginning,** state the topic and your opinion.

- In the **middle,** give reasons that support your opinion. Include facts and details that support each reason.

- At the **end,** give a concluding section that restates your opinion.

Provide Reasons

The middle part of your opinion piece takes the most planning. Thinking about your reasons will help you organize your ideas before you write. Follow these steps.

1. Brainstorm to make a list of the reasons that support your opinion.

2. Look back at your list. Choose the strongest reasons. Usually the strongest reasons are the ones you can support with facts and details.

3. Cross out reasons that are not related to your opinion. For example, here are two facts about more school days.

> RELATED TO THE OPINION: More days in school means more time to learn a subject.
>
> NOT RELATED TO THE OPINION: Some schools are making the school day longer.

Using a graphic organizer is a good way to plan and organize your ideas.

BEGINNING Opinion:	There should be more school days in the school year.
MIDDLE Reason 1:	Teachers would have more time to teach a subject.
Reason 2:	Students would not forget what they learned during long summer breaks.
Reason 3:	Students would have more time to study tough subjects.
END Conclusion:	The school year should be lengthened to improve students' education.

Use linking words and phrases, such as *because, therefore, in addition,* and *for example,* to help readers make connections between reasons or examples and your opinion.

Provide a Conclusion

Your **conclusion** is the last part of the opinion piece your reader will read. Summarize your main points. Be sure to use effective words that fit your audience.

Proofread Your Writing

Before others read your writing, check that your opinion piece is clear and your reasons are organized and easy to understand. Use the following checklist to write your final opinion piece.

- ☐ Do I begin with a clear topic and opinion?
- ☐ Do I give enough reasons to convince readers?
- ☐ Is the information presented in an organized way?
- ☐ Do I use linking words to make the ideas easy to follow?
- ☐ Do I use words that fit my audience?
- ☐ Does the writing use correct grammar and spelling?

Language Spotlight • Subject-Verb Agreement

In a sentence, the subject must always agree, or match, the verb in number. This is called **subject-verb agreement**. A singular subject takes a singular verb. Most singular verbs end with -s. A plural subject takes a plural verb.

Explain how you can tell that the subject and verb agree in each sentence below. Then write two more sentences to complete the chart. Make sure the subjects and verbs agree.

Singular Subject and Verb	Plural Subject and Verb
The girl *plays* in the yard.	The girls *play* in the yard.

Read the passage.

Is Recess an Important Part of the School Day?

For some students, recess is the best part of their school day. For other students, recess is a waste of time. Teachers, like students, also have different opinions about recess. I think that there are good reasons both for and against recess.

After a morning of hard work, students can't wait to take a break. Recess lets them relax. They are free to choose what to do. Some students choose to run or play games. Others just sit and talk with their friends. These students enjoy recess. It is an important part of the school day.

On the other hand, some students dislike recess. One reason is that they may not get along well with others. Recess usually takes place outdoors. Students are allowed to run around. They are not as well behaved as in a classroom. This free time makes problems more likely. When it is cold outside, students have another reason for disliking recess. It takes too much time to get in and out of warm clothes. During a thirty-minute recess, students may take fifteen minutes just getting dressed and undressed!

Like students, some teachers think recess is very important. Their reasons may differ from those of their students. For instance, students sit for a long time in the morning. This builds up extra energy. Teachers believe the students need a break. Without a break, they say, students get restless. They cannot focus. Their learning decreases. Teachers have seen that recess can help students get back to learning.

However, some teachers want to do away with recess. They want to use that time for helping students learn more in the classroom. Other teachers are afraid that students will get hurt when they play outdoors.

Deciding if recess is important is not easy. I think the reasons in favor of recess and against recess all make sense. In other words, students and teachers have good reasons for both opinions.

Answer the following questions.

1 This question has two parts. First, answer Part A. Then, answer Part B.

Part A

Which sentence **best** tells the author's opinion about recess?

A. All schools should have recess.

B. There are good reasons for and against recess.

C. Outdoor recess gives too much freedom to children.

D. Some teachers do not think students should have recess.

Part B

Which details from the passage support your answer to Part A? Write the sentences on the lines below.

_____

_____

_____

_____

_____

Hint For Part A, look in the introduction for the author's opinion. For Part B, reread the conclusion of the passage to see how the author sums up his or her opinion.

2 Circle **three** examples of linking words in the passage.

> **Hint** Remember, authors use linking words to connect opinions and reasons.

3 According to the passage, which sentences give reasons that students are in favor of recess? Circle **all** that apply.

A. After a morning of hard work, students can't wait to take a break.

B. Recess is very important to some students.

C. Recess lets students relax.

D. Without a break, students get restless.

E. Students are free to choose what to do.

F. Recess helps students get back to learning.

> **Hint** The question asks why students like recess. Focus on the part of the passage that gives the students' reasons.

4 The author wants to add the following sentence to the passage.

You should think about the different reasons before forming your own opinion.

Where in the passage is the **best** place to add this sentence?

A. at the end of paragraph 2

B. at the end of paragraph 3

C. at the end of paragraph 5

D. at the end of paragraph 6

> **Hint** Notice that the sentence refers to the many reasons that have been presented. Would it fit better at the beginning or end of the passage?

Use the Reading Guide to help you understand the passage.

Why We Need Recess

Reading Guide

How can you tell what the author thinks?

Notice how each paragraph focuses on a different reason to support the author's opinion.

How does the author back up the reasons for his or her opinion?

Most schools give students a break during the school day. This break, called recess, gives students time to play, have fun, or just relax. Not everyone believes recess is an important part of the school day. I do. I think recess can help both students and teachers in many ways.

Recess helps children learn skills they need in life. For instance, students learn how to cooperate, share, and take turns as they play. The Council on Physical Education for Children found that recess gives children the chance to practice problem-solving in real situations. Think of how important this skill is. Students have to solve problems every day when doing schoolwork.

Another benefit of recess is that it lowers stress. In the classroom, students are under pressure to perform well. They need to learn a great deal of information. They are then tested on what they have learned. This can cause them to feel stressed. However, when children take part in active play, their stress levels are reduced. Therefore, the physical activity they do at recess helps their minds as well.

A third reason students need recess is to keep their bodies fit. It makes sense that the more active someone is, the more fit he or she becomes. Without recess, students would spend hours sitting in one place. Some say that students get to exercise in gym class. However, gym class is not enough. Students need time to play on their own. They need some free time to burn off energy. Doctors and other experts have said that students need both gym class and recess for good health.

Look at the linking words at the beginning of the first three paragraphs on this page. How do linking words help make the information easier to understand?

Why does the author give a reason not to have recess? How does the author answer this reason?

What is the purpose of the last paragraph?

In addition to helping students' bodies and minds, recess can help improve test scores! Giving children time to talk and play with one another freely helps improve vocabulary. It has been shown that more free time in the school day can help children do better on tests. Both teachers and students would be happy to see higher test scores.

On the other hand, some teachers believe that recess takes too much time away from teaching. There are so many subjects to teach in one day. Time is already too short for teachers to get to everything they want to teach. Recess just makes it harder to complete the lessons of the day.

However, what good is having more time to teach if children are not learning? Recess can actually help children learn. Children need a break after working for a long time. When they take the break and then come back, the work seems new. Students are better able to focus after recess.

I don't believe recess is wasted time. I do not believe it takes away time from learning. If anything, I think the opposite is true. As I have shown, recess helps students and teachers alike. It is just one tool we can use to help students improve their bodies and their minds.

Answer the following questions.

1 This question has two parts. First, answer Part A. Then, answer Part B.

Part A

Which sentence **best** describes the author's opinion?

A. Recess can help improve teaching and learning.

B. Recess causes problems by taking time away from learning.

C. If students have gym class, they do not need recess.

D. When students return from recess, they will always do well on a test.

Part B

Find a sentence in the passage that **best** supports your answer to Part A. Write your answer on the lines provided.

_____

_____

_____

_____

_____

2 The following question has two parts. First, answer Part A. Then, answer Part B.

Part A

How is this passage organized?

A. main idea and details

B. time order

C. cause and effect

D. compare and contrast

Part B

Identify a paragraph that supports your answer to Part A. Explain how you can tell information is organized in the way you chose for Part A. Write your answer on the lines provided.

_____

_____

_____

_____

_____

_____

_____

_____

_____

_____

3 Read the following opinion some teachers have about recess.

> **On the other hand, some teachers believe that recess takes too much time away from teaching.**

Which reason from the text argues against this opinion?

A. There are so many subjects to teach in one day.

B. Students are better able to focus after recess.

C. Time is already too short for teachers to get to everything they want to teach.

D. Recess just makes it harder to complete the lessons of the day.

4 Reread the following paragraph from the passage and answer the question below.

> **However, what good is having more time to teach if children are not learning? Recess can actually help children learn. Children need a break after working for a long time. When they take the break and then come back, the work seems new. Students are better able to focus after recess.**

Which sentence is the **best** one to add to the end of this paragraph?

A. However, students will not have enough time.

B. For example, students may need more time to relax.

C. Therefore, students will learn more.

D. On the other hand, students may be tired.

5 Choose **two** sentences in which the subject and verb agree.

A. Most schools gives students a break during the school day.

B. They need to learn a great deal of information.

C. A student have to solve problems every day when doing schoolwork.

D. Recess just makes it harder to complete the lessons of the day.

6 The passage "Why We Need Recess" presents a student's opinion in favor of recess. Evaluate the passage. Write two to three paragraphs that tell whether you think the author included good reasons to back up his or her opinion. Discuss each reason and tell why you think it was or was not effective. Tell about anything the author could have added or done better. Be sure to include text evidence from the passage in your response.

You may plan your opinion piece in the space below. Write your opinion piece on the following pages.

Plan

Write your opinion piece on the lines below.

_____

_____

_____

_____

_____

_____

_____

_____

_____

_____

_____

_____

_____

_____

_____

_____

W.3.5, L.3.1.a, L.3.1.d–i, L.3.2.a, L.3.2.c, L.3.3.a

Revise and Edit

① GETTING THE IDEA

Good writers revise and edit their drafts to make them better.

Revising Your Work
When you **revise**, you read your draft carefully. You look to see if your ideas make sense. Then, you make changes to improve your draft.

Sentence Variety Use **sentence variety,** or a combination of sentence types to make your writing more interesting. A **simple sentence** expresses one complete thought. A **compound sentence** is made up of two or more simple sentences. A **complex sentence** includes a sentence that can stand alone and a group of words that cannot.

Read these two paragraphs. Which one has a better variety of sentences? Why does using different kinds of sentences make the writing more interesting?

> The Komodo dragon eats birds. This large lizard waits. Then it pounces on its prey. The Komodo dragon bites its prey. The poison from its fangs acts to kill the prey.

> The Komodo dragon eats birds. This large lizard waits, and then it pounces on its prey. When the Komodo dragon bites its prey, the poison from its fangs acts to kill the prey.

Reread the second paragraph. Underline the compound sentence. Circle the complex sentence.

Editing for Grammar

After you **revise** your draft, **edit** it for errors in grammar.

Conjunctions Use a **conjunction** to join or connect words or groups of words. A **coordinating conjunction** connects two or more words that are used in the same way, such as two subjects or two verbs. The coordinating conjunctions are *and, but, or, nor, for, so, yet*. A **subordinating conjunction** connects a subordinate clause to the rest of a sentence. Some examples are *after, although, as, because, before, if, since, unless, when*.

Circle the conjunction in each sentence below.

> After the snake bites its prey, the prey dies.
>
> The gray wolf is large and fierce.

Comparative and Superlative Adjectives and Adverbs

Adjectives describe people, places, and things (*old man, busy city, blue door*). Adverbs describe actions (*walk quickly, breathe deeply, try hard*). There are special forms of these words to use when making comparisons. Use the **comparative** form to compare two things. For example, "The dog is bigger than the puppy." Use the **superlative** form to compare three or more things: "Which boy in the class runs the fastest?" Check to see whether you need to change the spelling of the base word before you add the ending. Read the rules below.

- For all one-syllable words and many two-syllable words, add *-er* for the comparative and *-est* for the superlative: big, big**ger**, big**gest**

- For all three-syllable words and some two-syllable words, use *more* to form the comparative and *most* to form the superlative: delicious, **more** delicious, **most** delicious

Verb Tense A **verb** is a word that shows action. The **tense** of the verb tells the time when the action happens. The simple tenses are present, past, and future.

Most verbs are regular. Form the past tense by adding -*ed* to the present tense. Change the spelling of the base word if you need to. Some verbs are irregular. They do not use -*ed* to form the past tense. Look at the examples in the chart. Which verbs are regular? Which ones are irregular?

Present	Past	Future
I **walk** now.	I **walked** yesterday.	I **will walk** tomorrow.
I **hop** now.	I **hopped** yesterday.	I **will hop** tomorrow.
I **go** now.	I **went** yesterday.	I **will go** tomorrow.
I **say** now.	I **said** yesterday.	I **will say** tomorrow.
I **know** now.	I **knew** yesterday.	I **will know** tomorrow.

Subject-Verb Agreement A complete sentence has a subject – the one doing the action, and a verb – the kind of action. The subject and the verb in a sentence must agree, or match in number. This is called **subject-verb agreement**. A singular subject must have a singular verb. A plural subject must have a plural verb. How is the singular verb different from the plural verb in this example?

The boy **sings**.   The boys **sing**.

Pronoun-Antecedent Agreement A **pronoun** takes the place of a noun. A pronoun must agree with its antecedent. An **antecedent** is the noun that the pronoun replaces. A singular antecedent must have a singular pronoun. A plural antecedent must have a plural pronoun. Look at each example. How do you know that the pronoun and antecedent agree?

A **girl** packs **her** lunch.   The **girls** pack **their** lunch.

Proofreading Your Work

Proofread your work very carefully to spot errors.

Capitalize titles The **title** is the name of a story, article, or other piece of writing. Capitalize the first word and then only the important words in the rest of a title. Notice which words are capitalized in this example.

> the little house in the big woods
> The Little House in the Big Woods

Punctuate dialogue The words that the characters speak are called **dialogue.** Put quotation marks around the dialogue. Use a **comma** to separate the character's words from his or her name, after *said*.

> Julie said, "Let's go to the beach."

Form possessives A **possessive noun** shows ownership. For singular nouns, add an **apostrophe** *s*. For plural nouns, add an apostrophe to a plural noun ending in *s*.

> the boy**'s** bike   a class**'s** Web site
> the boys**'** bikes   two classes**'** Web site

Spell correctly Check your writing. Think about the spelling patterns and rules you know. Use print and digital dictionaries if you can. Ask your teacher or another student for help.

Spotlight Skill • Strong Words and Phrases

Strong words help readers form pictures in their minds. Choose strong words to describe things and to get your meaning across. Read the sentences below. Why is the second sentence better?

> The **big** bear **eats** other animals.

> The **enormous** bear **devours** other animals.

Now write your own sentence that uses strong words and phrases.

This passage contains mistakes. Read the passage.

Lucky and Lost Socks Island

(1) Lucky the athletic sock was happily sloshing around in the washing machine. (2) He was proud that Jake always wore him for his games.

(3) Lucky felt the washing machine shift into the spin cycle. (4) Suddenly, he went out along with the water. (5) He tumbled through a long, dark tube. (6) Finally, he plopped down on a beach.

(7) A group of sad-looking socks rushed up to him.

(8) "Where am I? (9) How did I get here?" sputtered Lucky.

(10) A rainbow-striped sock answered. (11) "You're on Lost Socks Island. (12) A magical water spout brought you here."

(13) Lucky stood up and shook off the sand. (14) He said, "I have to get home right now. (15) Jake needs me for the big game."

(16) "There's no way off the island," said a sock that had pictures of cats all over it.

(17) A purple and green polka-dotted sock added, "We have tried and tried. (18) We all want to go home."

(19) I will figure out a way Lucky said.

(20) The socks gave Lucky a tour of the small island. (21) Right away he noticed the tall coconut trees, plus some large pieces of driftwood.

(22) "We need to build a boat," he told them.

(23) "That's ridiculous," said a faded brown sock. (24) "We don't have an engine. (25) We'll get stuck on the ocean. (26) I would rather stay here. (27) At least we're safe."

(28) Lucky explained, "We'll use the driftwood for the boat. (29) I'll use strands of coconut fiber to sew all of you together to make a sail, and I will steer the boat."

(30) The socks all cheered, "Let's do it!"

(31) By the end of the day, the boat was ready. (32) Lucky pushed the boat into the water and raised the sock sail.

(33) The wind greeted them. (34) "Such a clever plan!" she said. (35) "I'll help you get home."

(36) In a few days the orange lookout sock called out, "Land ho!"

(37) The wind blew the little boat onto the beach. (38) Lucky took apart the sail. (39) The socks jumped up and down, cheering for Lucky.

(40) With a last mighty puff, the wind sent all of the socks back to their washing machines. (41) Lucky quickly plugged the magical waterspout in his machine so none of his friends would slip through it.

(42) Then, Jake looked in the dryer and pulled Lucky out. (43) "Whew, I thinked you were lost! (44) I don't know how I would play the big game without you."

(45) Lucky smiled to himself.

Answer the following questions.

1 This question has two parts. First, answer Part A. Then, answer Part B.

Part A

The verb in each sentence below is underlined. Which verb is the weakest?

A. Suddenly he <u>went</u> out along with the water.

B. He <u>tumbled</u> through a long, dark tube.

C. Finally, he <u>plopped</u> down on a beach.

D. A group of sad-looking socks <u>rushed</u> up to him.

Part B

Rewrite the sentence you chose in Part A using a stronger verb.

Write your answer on the lines below.

_____

_____

> **Hint** Think about the words *went*, *tumbled*, *plopped*, and *rushed*. Which words show actions that you can clearly picture in your mind? Which word does not?

2 This question has two parts. First, answer Part A. Then, answer Part B.

Part A

Read the paragraph from the passage.

> (23) "That's ridiculous," said a faded brown sock. (24) "We don't have an engine. (25) We'll get stuck on the ocean. (26) I would rather stay here. (27) At least we're safe."

What is a way to improve sentence variety in this paragraph? Circle **all** that apply.

A. Combine sentences 23 and 25.

B. Combine sentences 23 and 27.

C. Combine sentences 24 and 25.

D. Combine sentences 26 and 27.

Part B

Use conjunctions to combine the sentences you identified in Part A.

Write your answer on the lines below.

_____

_____

_____

_____

Hint There are a few short, choppy sentences in the paragraph. How can they be combined? Which connecting words would you use to combine them?

3 The following sentence contains errors in punctuation. Rewrite the sentence correctly.

I will figure out a way Lucky said.

_____

_____

> **Hint** What words does Lucky say? What punctuation should be added to set off his words?

4 The following question has two parts. First, answer Part A. Then, answer Part B.

Part A

Read the sentences from the passage and the directions that follow.

> **(40) With a last mighty puff, the wind sent all of the socks back to their washing machines. (41) Lucky quickly plugged the magical waterspout in his machine so none of his friends would slip through it.**

> **(42) Then, Jake looked in the dryer and pulled Lucky out. (43) "Whew, I thinked you were lost! (44) I don't know how I would play the big game without you."**

> **(45) Lucky smiled to himself.**

Circle the sentence that has an incorrect form of a verb.

Part B

Rewrite the sentence you chose in Part A so it is correct.

Write your answer on the lines below.

_____

_____

> **Hint** This question has two parts. First, read each sentence carefully. Look for the verbs, or action words. Which sentence has a verb that doesn't sound right to your ears? Then, rewrite the sentence correctly.

The passage contains mistakes. Use the Reading Guide to help you find the mistakes and understand the passage.

The Smallest and Largest Frogs in the World

Reading Guide

In sentence 5, the word *smallest* is a superlative adjective. It is used to compare the newly discovered frog to other frogs.

Notice how the first word in each sentence is capitalized. In sentence 10, *New Guinea* is also capitalized because it is the name of a country.

Find the word *they* in sentence 19. Who does the word *they* refer to in the sentence?

The Smallest Frog in the World

(1) Just a few years ago, scientists discovered the world's tiniest known <u>frog</u>. (2) It is only about a quarter inch long. (3) That is about the size of a housefly. (4) The miniature frog would easily fit on your fingernail. (5) In addition to being the smallest frog, it is also the world's smallest four-legged vertebrate, or animal with a backbone. (6) Scientists wrote about it in the article "the discovery of the world's smallest vertebrate."

(7) Around the same time, scientists found a slightly larger frog in the same place. (8) This one was about one-third inch long. (9) That is about the size of a bumblebee. (10) The tiny frogs were found on the island of New Guinea. (11) The frogs live on the moist rain forest floor in the mountains there.

(12) As you can imagine, it was very hard to find these miniature creatures. (13) Its size makes the frogs hard to see. (14) Their earth-colored skin patterns act as camouflage. (15) They blend in with the leaf litter.

(16) Scientists listened for the frogs. (17) The frogs don't croak like larger frogs. (18) Instead, they make a high-pitched sound, especially at dawn and dusk. (19) Once the scientists thought they had located the sound, they scooped a big pile of leaf litter into a bag. (20) Then, they carefully inspected it. (21) When something moved, they knew they had seen a teeny frog. (22) The scientists took pictures of the frogs. (23) Later, they used the zoom lens of the camera to see the frogs up close.

Reading Guide

Does the author use a good variety of sentences? Which sentences would you change? Why?

Is all the punctuation and spelling correct? How do you know?

(24) The mini-frogs are great jumpers. (25) They can jump up to nine inches. (26) That is a very long distance for such a small animal.

(27) What does such a small animal eat? (28) Smaller animals! (29) The mini-frogs eat mites. (30) Mites are about the size of a pin head. (31) Larger animals don't eat mites, so there is plenty of food for the mini-frogs.

(32) Scientists will continue to study the mini-frogs and learn more about them. (33) Some scientists think there are even more species of mini-frogs. (34) They'll keep their eyes on the leaf litter to find out!

The Largest Frog in the World

(35) The Goliath frog is the world's <u>enormous</u> frog species. (36) With its legs tucked under its body, an adult Goliath frog is about twelve and a half inches long. (37) When stretched out, it measures up to thirty inches from end to end. (38) It weighs up to seven pounds. (39) That's the size of a small cat! (40) The top of the frog is green, while the underside is yellow-orange.

(41) Goliath frogs live in just one place in the world. (42) Their habitat is the rain forests of western Africa. (43) They like to be near rivers and waterfalls. (44) These huge frogs eat insects, fish, crabs, and other amphibians.

(45) Because of its huge size, the Goliath frog does not hop very far. (46) It moves slowly, and stops after just a few hops. (47) Unlike other frogs, the Goliath frog does not croak or make any other noises.

(48) Goliath frogs are endangered. (49) Local people hunt them for food because they say the frogs meat is delicious. (50) Hunters sells the frogs to zoos or pet stores. (51) Sadly, the frogs don't last long out of their native habitats. (52) Logging and farming are destroying their habitat. (53) If the rain forests are completely cleared, the frogs will probably die out.

Answer the following questions.

1 Read the sentence from the passage. Then, answer the question below.

The Goliath frog is the world's <u>enormous</u> frog species.

What is the correct way to write the superlative form of the word <u>enormous</u>?

A. enormouser

B. more enormous

C. most enormous

D. enormousest

2 The following question has two parts. First, answer Part A. Then, answer Part B.

Part A

Which sentence has an error in subject-verb agreement?

A. They blend in with the leaf litter.

B. Hunters sells the frogs to zoos or pet stores.

C. These huge frogs eat insects, fish, crabs, and other amphibians.

D. Scientists listened for the frogs.

Part B

Rewrite the sentence you chose in Part A so it is correct. Write your answer on the lines below.

_____

_____

_____

_____

3 What is the correct way to capitalize the title in the sentence below?

The scientists wrote about it in the article "the discovery of the world's smallest vertebrate."

A. "The Discovery Of The World's Smallest Vertebrate"

B. "The discovery of the world's smallest vertebrate"

C. "The Discovery of the World's Smallest Vertebrate"

D. "The Discovery of The World's Smallest Vertebrate"

4 The following question has two parts. First, answer Part A. Then, answer Part B.

Part A

Read this paragraph from the passage and the directions that follow.

(12) As you can imagine, it was very hard to find these miniature creatures. (13) Its size makes the frogs hard to see. (14) Their earth-colored skin patterns act as camouflage. (15) They blend in with the leaf litter.

Circle the sentence that has an error in pronoun-antecedent agreement.

Part B

Which pronoun should replace the incorrect pronoun in the sentence you circled?

A. my

B. his

C. our

D. their

5 Read both parts of the question before responding.

Part A

Read the sentences from the passage. Which sentence should use the possessive form of the word <u>frog</u>?

A. The tiny frogs were found on the island of New Guinea.

B. Goliath frogs live in just one place in the world.

C. Local people hunt them for food because they say the frogs meat is delicious.

D. If the rain forests are completely cleared, the frogs will probably die out.

Part B

Rewrite the sentence you chose in Part A so it is correct.

_____

_____

_____

6 Reread the passage "The Smallest and Largest Frogs in the World." Then, write two or three paragraphs to compare and contrast the two frog species. Use details from the passage to help you compare and contrast what the frogs look like, where they live, and what they eat.

Use a variety of sentences in your writing. Include comparative and superlative adjectives, and choose strong words and phrases for effect.

When you are finished, be sure to check that you have followed the rules of grammar, punctuation, capitalization, and spelling.

You may plan your paragraphs in the space below. Then, write your response on the following pages.

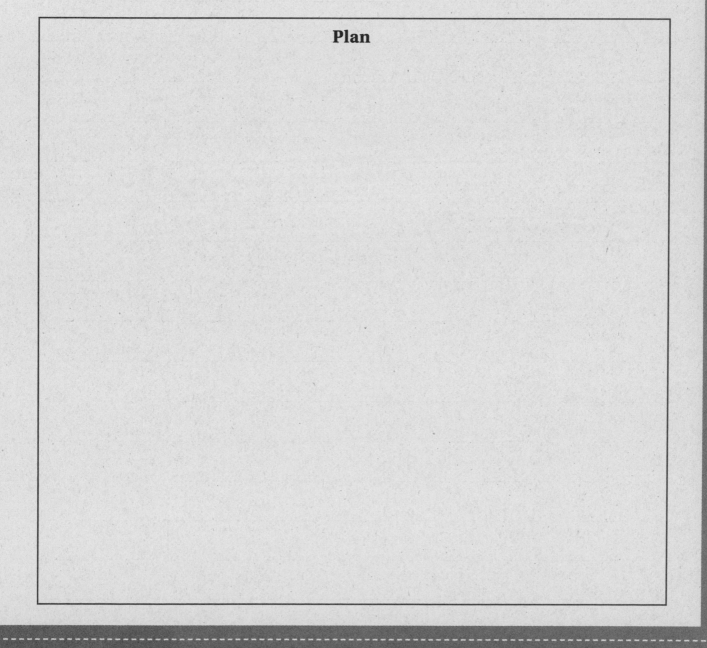

Plan

Write your response on the lines below.

_____

_____

_____

_____

_____

_____

_____

_____

_____

_____

_____

_____

_____

_____

_____

_____

_____

Read the passage.

excerpted from

Letters to His Children

by Theodore Roosevelt

Theodore Roosevelt was the president of the United States from 1901 to 1909. He was also the father of six children: Alice, Ted, Kermit, Quentin, Archie, and Ethel. Roosevelt's job meant that he was often away from his children. To stay in touch, he wrote them dozens of letters. In 1919, many of the letters were published in a book.

Roosevelt wrote this letter to Quentin during a trip to California. He describes what it was like to be away from home.

Del Monte, California, May 10, 1903

DEAREST QUENTY-QUEE:

I loved your letter. I am very homesick for Mother and for you children; but I have enjoyed this week's travel. I have been among the orange groves, where the trees have oranges growing thick upon them, and there are more flowers than you have ever seen . . . . Whenever I see a little boy being brought up by his father or mother to look at the procession as we pass by, I think of you and Archie and feel very homesick. Sometimes little boys ride in the procession on their ponies, just like Archie on Algonquin.

Roosevelt's children sometimes traveled from the White House, too. Roosevelt wrote this letter to Ted, who was away at school. He describes life at the White House.

White House, May 28, 1904

DEAR TED:

Life is lovely here. The country is beautiful, and I do not think that any two people ever got more enjoyment out of the White House than Mother and I. We love the house itself. . . . We love the garden. And we like Washington. We almost always take our breakfast on the south portico. Then we stroll about the garden for fifteen or twenty minutes, looking at the flowers and the fountain and admiring the trees. Then I work until between four and five. If Mother wants to ride, we then spend a couple of hours on horseback.

In this letter to Kermit, Roosevelt talks about winter in the White House.

White House, December 17, 1904

BLESSED KERMIT:

For a week the weather has been cold—down to zero at night and rarely above freezing in the shade at noon. . . . I have been so busy that I have been unable to get away until after dark, but I went in the fur jacket Uncle Will presented to me . . ., and the moonlight on the glittering snow made the rides lovelier than they would have been in the daytime. Sometimes Mother and Ted went with me, and the gallops were delightful. Today it has snowed heavily again, but the snow has been so soft that I did not like to go out, and besides I have been worked up to the limit. There has been skating and sleigh-riding all the week . . . .

In this letter, the president updates Quentin on the family's cat, Slippers. He also talks about how much he misses his family when they are away.

White House, April 1, 1906

DARLING QUENTY-QUEE:

Slippers and the kittens are doing finely. I think the kittens will be big enough for you to pet and have some satisfaction out of when you get home . . . . The house feels big and lonely and full of echoes with nobody but me in it; and I do not hear any small scamps running up and down the hall just as hard as they can; or hear their voices while I am dressing; or suddenly look out through the windows of the office at the tennis ground and see them racing over it . . . . I love you very much.

Answer the following questions.

1 This question has two parts. First, answer Part A. Then, answer Part B.

Part A

Which sentence **best** states Roosevelt's opinion about living in the White House when his children are not there?

A. It is fun to play in the snow and on the grounds.

B. The grounds are beautiful year-round.

C. It is too quiet.

D. The kittens provide company.

Part B

Underline **one** detail from the passage that supports your response to Part A.

2 This question has two parts. First, answer Part A. Then, answer Part B.

Part A

Read the sentence from the passage. Underline the conjunctions in the sentence.

> **Today it has snowed heavily again, but the snow has been so soft that I did not like to go out, and besides I have been worked up to the limit.**

Part B

Choose one of the conjunctions you identified in Part A. On the lines, describe how it connects ideas in the sentence.

_____

_____

_____

3 Read all parts of the question before responding.

Part A

A student has written the following sentences for a report about Theodore Roosevelt's children. Circle the sentence that would make the best topic sentence. Cross out the sentence that would not belong in the report.

> **Theodore Roosevelt had six children.**
>
> **Roosevelt's oldest child, Alice, was born in 1884.**
>
> **The teddy bear was named after Roosevelt.**
>
> **Roosevelt enjoyed spending time with his children at the White House.**
>
> **Roosevelt's youngest son, Quentin, was killed during World War I.**

Part B

What additional information might the student include in the report? Choose **all** that apply.

A. laws that were passed while Roosevelt was president

B. ages of Roosevelt's children when they lived in the White House

C. why a national park was named after Theodore Roosevelt

D. description of his daughter Alice's wedding at the White House

E. names of the Roosevelt children's pets

F. information about Roosevelt's early years as president

Part C

Underline **one** detail from the passage that the student might include in the report.

Read the passage.

Growing Up in the White House

Our country's presidents are not the only people who have lived in the White House. Children have lived there, too. The granddaughter of John Adams was the first child to live in the White House. More recently, Barack Obama's daughters, Sasha and Malia, live there.

Being a "first kid" can be fun. But living in the White House with a parent as president can be hard at times, too.

White House Lives

Children in the White House do many of the same things you do. They play games. They have friends spend the night. They have swim parties at the White House pool and play baseball on the lawn. They bowl in the bowling alley and watch movies in the movie theater. Sometimes they even go on trips with their families. George W. Bush's daughters, Barbara and Jenna, went to Africa with their parents.

In other ways, the lives of presidents' children are very different from those of other kids. First kids must have a security person with them at all times to keep them safe. And even though White House children get to go to many events, they may not always want to do so. Some people did not like it when President Jimmy Carter's daughter, Amy, read a book during a fancy dinner. When she wanted to be alone, Amy often went to the tree house built behind the White House.

Just like you, kids in the White House go to school. However, their school experiences can look very different. Abraham Lincoln's son, Tad, had a private tutor come to the White House. John F. Kennedy's daughter, Caroline, went to first grade in the White House, too. Her parents set up a classroom on the third floor for Caroline and ten other children. Amy Carter attended public school. President Bill Clinton's daughter, Chelsea, went to a private school.

Family Pets

The White House has seen its share of first pets. President Barack Obama's family has two dogs, Bo and Sunny. They go for walks and sometimes greet people touring the White House. President Bush's dog, Barney, could be viewed on a webcam on the White House Web site. President Kennedy's family brought two hamsters, a cat, and a bird to the White House. They added ponies and a dog while living there.

Theodore Roosevelt's children brought many pets to the White House. They had cats, dogs, a snake, a raccoon, a bird, and a pony named Algonquin. When Archie Roosevelt was sick one day, his brother, Quentin, snuck the pony into the White House to cheer him up. Algonquin and Quentin rode the elevator up to Archie's room!

Fun at Home

Many presidents' children have used the White House as a giant playground. The Roosevelt children played leapfrog and climbed on the furniture. They crawled through the spaces between the ceilings and floors. They even roller-skated and rode bikes in the White House. They also did quiet things like reading in the White House library.

President Kennedy's son, John, loved to play hide-and-seek. His father even had a secret door made in his desk so John could hide in his office. While playing outside one day, John fell into a fountain on the White House lawn. The fountain was full of mud, and his mother also fell in while trying to help her son. Someone then had to throw a rope to the first lady and her son to get them out of the fountain. Just another everyday adventure at the White House!

Answer the following questions.

4 This question has two parts. First, answer Part A. Then, answer Part B.

Part A

Based on the the passage "Growing Up in the White House," which of the following statements is true?

A. All presidents' children have enjoyed living in the White House.

B. All presidents' children have had pets in the White House.

C. Presidents' children need protection to stay safe.

D. Presidents' children do better in school than other children.

Part B

Underline a detail from the passage that **best** supports your response to Part A.

5 The following question has two parts. First, answer Part A. Then, answer Part B.

Part A

Tessa is doing additional research for a report on the children of President John F. Kennedy. Circle the two **best** sources for information that relates to her topic.

Research Sources	a biography about John F. Kennedy and his family
	the White House Web site, www.whitehouse.gov
	a blog about a student's visit to the Kennedy library
	a fictional story about the Kennedy children's pony

Part B

Explain why the sources you chose in Part A are the most useful.

_____

_____

_____

_____

6 Read all parts of the question before responding.

Part A

Jamal decided to write a story about the Roosevelt children and their pony, Algonquin. The following sentences from Jamal's story contain mistakes. Rewrite each sentence correctly on the lines.

A. One day Quentins brother Archie was sick in bed.

_____

B. I'll bet seeing Algonquin will make Archie feel best, said Quentin.

_____

C. Quentin knowed it would be hard to lead a pony up the stares.

_____

D. He takes the elevater instead.

_____

E. People still laughs at the funny story of a pony in the white house.

_____

Part B

Combine your revisions of sentences C and D from Part A into one sentence. Remember to use a conjunction to link both parts of the sentence. Write the new sentence on the line.

_____

_____

Part C

Underline the verb and circle the adjective in your revision of sentence E. Then rewrite the sentence using a stronger verb and adjective.

_____

_____

PERFORMANCE TASK

In "Letters to His Children" and "Growing Up in the White House," you learned what it might be like to live in the White House with one of your parents serving as the president of the United States. Write an essay that states whether or not you would want to have that experience. Consider the following points:

- What are the positive things about being a first kid? What are the negative things?

- How would living in the White House change your life? Can you think of a personal experience you've had that might be similar?

Remember to use evidence from both passages to support your opinion.

You may plan your essay in the space below. Write your essay on the following pages.

Plan

Write your essay on the lines below.

STRAND 4

Listening

Listen to Stories

❶ GETTING THE IDEA

Do you enjoy listening to stories? Most students do. The purpose of reading a story aloud is to entertain the listeners.

Listening to a Story

When your teacher or librarian reads a story to you, you need to listen carefully. Sometimes, the reader will be directly in front of you. Or your teacher may use a computer to play a recording or to show a video presentation.

Purpose No matter how the story is presented, your purpose for listening is the same.

- Find out the **characters**, **setting**, and **plot**.

- Identify the **key details**.

- After the story is over, be ready to **summarize** the plot in just a few sentences.

- Tell the **theme**, which is the central message or lesson of the story.

Taking Notes Take notes to help you remember what you heard. Jot down names, places, and key words and ideas. Draw pictures, too. They can help you remember connections between characters and plot events.

Visuals Visuals can be an important part of a story. These can include illustrations, photos, maps, charts, and diagrams. For example, if you were listening to the story "Cinderella," an illustration of the fairy godmother would help you understand what she might look like.

If your teacher is reading a story aloud to the class, he or she may read it twice. Each time, listen for different things.

First Listen

The first time you listen to a story, take notes on the important elements. Jot down the name of the main character, the setting, and the problem and solution in the plot. You might want to draw a story map that shows the beginning, middle, and end. Fill it in as you listen. Don't try to write down everything. But do write down any questions you have. During the second listen, listen for the answers to your questions.

Use this chart as a guide to the first listen.

First Listen		
Story Elements	**Ask Yourself**	**Listen For**
main character	Who is this story mostly about?	• the character's name • words that describe the character • words that the character says and things the character does that give clues about what the character is like
setting	When and where does this story take place?	• place names and descriptions • dates and time-order words and phrases, such as *this morning*, *yesterday*, *last year* • clues that suggest a different time period
plot	What happens in the story?	• clues about the character's problem, or the conflict, and how it is solved
genre, or kind of story	What kind of story is this?	• details that show whether this story could happen in real life or not

Second Listen

On your second listen, pay attention to story details. Look over your notes and review any questions. If you started a story map, return to it to take additional notes.

Listen for details that show how the characters and setting affect the plot. Ask yourself:

- What does the main character want?

- Who are the other characters?

- Is the setting important to the plot? How?

- How do the actions of all the characters move the story along?

- How does the main character try to solve the problem? What happens?

After Listening to the Story

Summarize the story in your own words. Write the summary in your notes. That will help you remember the most important parts. Then, think about the central message of the story. What lesson does the author want the reader to understand?

Language Spotlight • Use Glossaries or Dictionaries

Glossaries and dictionaries are word resources. A **glossary** is a list at the end of a text that gives the meanings of certain terms in the text. A **dictionary** gives the meanings of many words. You can use print and online glossaries and dictionaries to find or clarify the exact meaning of a word.

Read the following sentence.

The bus climbed up a steep grade.

What meanings of the word *grade* do you know? What might the word *grade* mean in the sentence above? Use a dictionary to confirm the meaning as it relates to this sentence.

Listen to the passage your teacher reads aloud and look at the picture. Take notes in the space below.

A Beautiful Idea

Notes

Answer the following questions.

1 Which sentence tells the problem in the story?

A. The winning idea would become a guide for their community service project.

B. Hannah already knew what some of her friends had in mind.

C. The assignment was due tomorrow, but Hannah still had no idea what she should suggest.

D. At first, the plants looked lonely sitting so far apart from each other.

> **Hint** The problem is an issue that the main character needs to solve.

2 The following question has two parts. First, answer Part A. Then, answer Part B.

Part A

What can you tell about the setting? Circle **all** that apply.

A. It takes place in the present.

B. It takes place at Hannah's home and school.

C. It takes place in the future.

D. It takes place in a country far away.

Part B

Choose one of the sentences you circled in Part A. Write one or two sentences that explain how you know these details about the setting. Use details from your notes to support your answer.

_____

_____

> **Hint** Which clues tell you where Hannah is? Think about whether there are any clues about a different time period or a different country. What conclusions can you draw from the details you heard?

3 Look at the picture on page 271. How does it help you better understand the passage? Circle **all** that apply.

A. It shows the story's message.

B. It shows the main character of the story.

C. It shows a key event in the plot.

D. It shows the problem in the story.

Hint What is happening in the picture? What story elements are shown?

4 Write two or three sentences to summarize this passage.

_____

_____

_____

_____

_____

Hint A summary should tell only the most important parts of the story in your own words.

Use the Listening Guide to help you understand the passage your teacher reads aloud. Take notes in the space below.

A Spark of Fire

Listening Guide

Look at the photograph on this page. What clues does it give about the setting of the story?

What is the story mostly about? Who are the main characters?

What is the problem in the story? How is the problem solved at the end?

Notes

Answer the following questions.

1 Read both parts of the question before responding.

Part A

Which statement **best** describes this passage?

A. It is a realistic story that takes place today.

B. It is a realistic story that takes place in the past.

C. It is a fantasy story that takes place in the future.

D. It is a fantasy story that takes place in an imaginary world.

Part B

Look at your answer in Part A, and look at the photograph on page 274. Write two or three sentences that support your response in Part A.

_____

_____

_____

_____

2 Ben Franklin believes that preventing fires is at least as important as putting them out. Which sentence from the passage **best** supports this idea?

A. "My friend Ben Franklin is forming a club of active men whose business it is to attend all fires whenever they happen."

B. "An ounce of prevention is worth a pound of cure," Mr. Franklin said.

C. Mr. Franklin spoke of the urgent need to help Philadelphians protect themselves from fire.

D. "Fire buckets should already be in every home," Mr. Franklin said.

3 Read the sentences and the questions that follow.

> **"I would advise people to take care how they carry <u>live</u> coals in a full shovel. Scraps of fire may fall into cracks and make no appearance until midnight."**

Part A

As it is used in the passage, what does the word <u>live</u> mean?

A. hot and glowing

B. having life

C. working

D. occupying a home

Part B

Which resource could you use to check the meaning of <u>live</u>? Circle **all** that apply.

A. an online dictionary

B. a print dictionary

C. an online encyclopedia

D. a print encyclopedia

4 Select **three** details from the passage that tell what the Union Fire Company plans to do to help the people of Philadelphia protect themselves from fire.

A. show people ways to prevent fire

B. meet with Ben Franklin

C. put fire buckets in every home

D. force people to leap out of windows during a fire

E. stop people from cooking in open fireplaces

F. fight fires

5 Write at least one paragraph that describes how the setting of "A Spark of Fire" affects the plot of the story. How do the time and place where the story takes place affect what the characters do? Use details from your notes and the photograph on page 274 to support your response.

Write your response on the lines below.

_____

_____

_____

_____

_____

_____

_____

_____

_____

_____

_____

_____

_____

_____

_____

_____

SL.3.2, SL.3.3, L.3.1.g

Listen to Presentations

① GETTING THE IDEA

A **presentation** is a talk or speech. Its purpose is to give information or to share an opinion. A presentation might be a firefighter talking about fire safety at a school assembly. It might be a classmate giving a report about Mexico.

Listening to a Presentation
When someone gives a presentation, it is important to pay attention and to listen carefully. Sometimes, the speaker will be in front of you. At other times, you may listen to an audio recording or watch a presentation online.

Purpose When you listen to a presentation, your purpose is always the same.

- Listen to find out the **main idea** or the speaker's opinion.

- Listen to identify the **details** the speaker gives to back up the main idea or the opinion.

Taking Notes You can take notes to help you remember what you hear. When you take notes, don't write down everything you hear. Instead, follow these tips.

- Write down key words and phrases.

- Write each new idea on a new line.

- Write quickly but neatly enough so you can read your notes later.

- Try to keep listening while you take notes.

Visuals Many presentations include **visuals** to help you understand a presentation or give new information. Maps, charts, diagrams, and photographs are some visuals that might be included with a presentation.

If your teacher is reading a presentation, he or she may read it twice. Each time you listen, you can understand it better if you listen for different things.

First Listen

The first time you listen, listen for the main idea. Take notes on the main idea, and write down any questions you have. During the second listen, you can listen for details and for the answers to your questions.

What is the main idea? A presentation is a lot like a nonfiction article. It always has a main idea that tells what the presentation is mostly about. Often the main idea is stated at the beginning of the presentation. For example, in a presentation about fire safety, the main idea might be "It is important to have a home fire safety plan." In a presentation about Mexico, the main idea might be "Mexico is a country with many different landforms." In a good presentation, the speaker will also restate the main idea at the end.

What is the structure? Nonfiction articles have different ways of organizing information to help readers connect ideas. A good presentation has structure, too. Listen for signal words that will help you connect ideas in the presentation.

Structure	Ask yourself	Listen for
sequence	Does the presentation tell about a series of events? Does it explain a process?	dates; signal words, such as *first*, *then*, *next*, *last*
cause and effect	What events happen? How do they cause other events to happen?	signal words, such as *because*, *cause*, *so*, *therefore*
problem and solution	Is there a problem to solve? Does the presentation offer solutions?	signal words, such as *problem*, *challenge*, *solution*, *action*
compare and contrast	Does the presentation explain how things are alike and different?	signal words, such as *alike*, *same*, *both*, *different*, *however*

Second Listen

Before you listen a second time, look over your notes and questions. Think about the main idea and the structure of the presentation. Write down any additional questions you have.

During the second listen, listen for reasons and evidence that support the main idea or opinion. Use what you know about the structure to help you connect the details to the main idea.

After the Presentation

After the presentation, **summarize** it in your own words. Use your notes to help you. Summarizing the presentation will help you remember the main idea and key details. It will also help you talk about the presentation with your classmates.

Language Spotlight • Comparative and Superlative Adjectives and Adverbs

An adjective is a word that describes a noun. An adverb is a word that describes a verb. Adjectives and adverbs can also be used to compare and contrast two or more things.

Comparative adjectives and adverbs compare two things.

- Ed is <u>taller</u> than Ann. (adjective)
- Ed arrives <u>earlier</u> than Ann. (adverb)
- Ed speaks <u>more softly</u> than Ann. (adverb)

Superlative adjectives and adverbs compare three or more things.

- Ed is the <u>tallest</u> kid in the class. (adjective)
- Ed arrives <u>earliest</u> of all. (adverb)
- Ed speaks <u>most softly</u> of all. (adverb)

Add the correct ending to the word *big* to complete each sentence.

Dad's shoes are _____ than my shoes.

Dad has the _____ shoes in the family.

Listen to the presentation your teacher reads aloud and study the photograph. Take notes in the space below.

The Amazing Venus Flytrap

Notes

Answer the following questions.

1 This question has two parts. First, answer Part A. Then, answer Part B.

Part A

What is the main idea of the presentation?

Write your answer on the lines below.

_____

_____

Part B

Which detail from the presentation does **not** support the main idea?

A. You have probably seen an insect eat a plant.

B. The two halves of the leaves snap shut, like jaws.

C. Then, special fluids inside the leaves break down the prey so the plant can digest the nutrients.

D. After a few days, the trap slowly reopens.

> **Hint** The main idea is what the presentation is mostly about. The supporting details explain the main idea.

2 What do the special fluids inside the Venus flytrap's leaves do?

A. make the leaves close

B. attract more insects

C. help the plant digest the insect

D. take in nutrients from the soil

> **Hint** Reread your notes. What did you write about how the plants use these fluids?

3 Read this paragraph from the presentation and follow the directions below.

> **You have probably seen an insect eat a plant. But have you ever seen a plant eat an insect? It really does happen, and it's one of the strangest sights you will ever see. One plant that eats insects is the Venus flytrap.**

Underline the superlative adjective.

> **Hint** An adjective is a descriptive word. In the paragraph, find an adjective that compares or contrasts more than two things. Look at the letters at the end of the adjective to give you a clue.

4 According to the presentation, why did the Venus flytrap have to adapt in order to survive? Include at least two details from the presentation to explain your answer.

Write your answer on the lines below.

_____

_____

_____

_____

_____

_____

> **Hint** Recall what you learned about the soil in places where Venus flytraps live.

Use the Listening Guide to help you understand the presentation your teacher reads aloud and study the photographs and the chart. Take notes in the space below.

Listening Guide

What is the main idea of the presentation?

What does the word *carnivorous* mean?

What plants are named in the presentation? How does each one catch its prey?

How do the photographs help you understand how each plant traps prey?

Carnivorous Plants

Pitcher plant

Sundew

Plant	How It Catches Prey
Venus flytrap	leaves snap shut
bladderwort	bladder with trap door that closes
pitcher plant	pitcher-shaped leaves with sticky hairs inside
sundew	sticky, spiky flowers

Notes

Answer the following questions.

1 What is the main idea of this presentation? Write a summary in your own words.

Write your answer on the lines below.

_____

_____

_____

_____

2 How does a sundew catch its prey?

A. with a spiky leaf that snaps shut

B. in a pitcher-shaped leaf full of nectar

C. with sticky gel

D. in a sac with a trapdoor

3 Which question about bladderworts is **not** answered in the presentation?

A. Where do bladderworts live?

B. How do bladderworts catch food?

C. What do bladderworts eat?

D. How much do bladderworts eat?

4 How does the chart on page 284 add to the presentation? Circle **all** that apply.

    A. It shows what some of the plants look like.

    B. It summarizes how some plants catch their prey.

    C. It explains why some plants eat insects.

    D. It names the meat-eating plants in the presentation.

5 The following question has two parts. First, answer Part A. Then, answer Part B.

Part A

Read this sentence from the presentation.

> **The Venus flytrap, for example, looks a little like a hairy, spiky bean.**

Which question could a listener ask about this sentence?

    A. What does the Venus flytrap eat?

    B. How does the Venus flytrap digest food?

    C. What part of the Venus flytrap looks like a bean?

    D. How does a Venus flytrap catch its prey?

Part B

Circle the answer to the question you chose in Part A.

    A. The leaves look like a hairy, spiky bean when they snap shut.

    B. Venus flytraps eat insects.

    C. The leaves snap shut around the prey.

    D. Chemicals inside the leaves help the plant digest the prey.

6 Choose one plant from the presentation to write about. Tell why you chose this plant and how it is similar to and different from the other meat-eating plants you learned about in the presentation.

Give evidence from the presentation to support your response.

Write your answer on the lines below.

_____

_____

_____

_____

_____

_____

_____

_____

_____

_____

_____

_____

_____

_____

Listen to the passage your teacher reads aloud. Take notes about the characters, setting, and plot events in the space below. Then answer the questions.

Notes

Answer the following questions.

1 Which sentence from the passage **best** describes an action Terrance takes in response to a problem?

    A. Terrance watched out the window as his mother walked down the street.

    B. He, too, would watch for ways to make things better for others.

    C. Terrance soon discovered that it was easy to find ways to help!

    D. The bus driver nodded a thank you.

2 The following question has two parts. First, answer Part A. Then, answer Part B.

Part A

Circle the type of fiction that **best** describes the passage.

folktale	fantasy story
myth	realistic story

Part B

Using your notes, list **three** details about the characters, setting, or plot events that support your answer to Part A.

_____

_____

_____

_____

_____

3 The words on the left describe Terrance's feelings. Draw lines to match Terrance's feelings to the story events that caused them.

A. proud

B. excited

C. puzzled

1. She put on her jacket and then pulled on rubber gloves and grabbed a trash bag.

2. Every so often, she picked up trash and put it in her bag.

3. Terrance smiled at himself in his mirror and hurried to find his mother.

4 Use your notes to write two or three sentences that summarize the passage.

_____

_____

_____

_____

5 This question has two parts. First, answer Part A. Then, answer Part B.

Part A

Which **best** states the central message of the passage?

A. Picking up trash is good for the environment.

B. It is important to help other people out.

C. It feels good to do things for others.

D. Kids should follow their parents' example.

Part B

Choose **three** details from the passage that support your answer to Part A.

A. Terrance wakes up early.

B. Terrance feels proud of his mom for picking up trash.

C. Terrance smiles after moving the loose rocks.

D. The bus driver nods a thank you to Terrance.

E. Terrance watches his mom out the window.

F. Terrance can't wait to tell his mom about his day.

Listen to the presentation your teacher reads aloud and look at the photographs. Pay attention to the main idea and supporting details. Take notes on the presentation in the space below. Then answer the questions.

How Adaptations Help Animals and Plants Survive

Arctic foxes have adapted to their surroundings by changing their fur color at different times of the year. In winter, their fur is white. In summer, it turns brown.

Notes

6 Summarize the main idea of the presentation on the lines below.

_____

_____

_____

7 The following question has two parts. First, answer Part A. Then, answer Part B.

Part A

Read each question in the box. Decide whether or not it was answered in the presentation. Write the question in the correct column in the chart.

What do koala bears eat?	What does skunk cabbage smell like?
What do arctic foxes hunt?	
Where do koala bears live?	What adaptation do arctic foxes have?
What does skunk cabbage taste like?	Why does prairie grass have long roots?
Why is it windy on the prairie?	

Answered	Not Answered

Part B

Choose one question you listed in the left-hand column. Use details from your notes to answer it. Write the answer on the line below.

_____

8 The following question has two parts. First, answer Part A. Then, answer Part B.

Part A

Read the sentence.

The weather is _____ when arctic foxes are white than when they are brown.

Which word or phrase completes the sentence correctly?

A. colder

B. coldest

C. more colder

D. most coldest

Part B

In what way do the photographs on page 292 **best** support the sentence in Part A?

A. They show that arctic foxes live in cold areas.

B. They show that arctic foxes are white when it is cold and snowy.

C. They show that arctic foxes do not like the cold.

D. They show that arctic foxes live by themselves.

9 Which of the following sentences **best** tells how the presentation is organized?

A. The presentation describes the process of developing an adaptation.

B. The presentation explains what causes an adaptation to develop.

C. The presentation gives information about different kinds of adaptations.

D. The presentation tells how adaptations are alike and different.

What is an adaptation? Describe one plant or animal adaptation that you learned about from the presentation. Tell how the adaptation helps the plant or animal to live. Use details from the presentation in your response.

Write your response on the lines below.

_____

_____

_____

_____

_____

_____

_____

_____

_____

_____

_____

_____

_____

_____

GLOSSARY

academic vocabulary the words that apply to general subjects, such as social studies and math, that help you understand the subjects (Lesson 6)

act one of the largest parts of a drama, or play; sometimes made up of scenes (Lesson 3)

affix the word part added to the beginning or ending of a root word that changes the meaning of the word (Lesson 3)

antecedent the noun that its pronoun, used later in the sentence, refers to (Lesson 17)

article a piece of writing online or in a magazine or newspaper (Lesson 5)

bibliography a list of the resources used for a written project (Lesson 14)

biography the true story of a person's life as told by someone else (Lesson 5)

caption a phrase or sentence that tells what a picture, image, or diagram is about; sometimes called a *label* (Lessons 5, 15)

cast the characters in a drama (Lesson 3)

cast of characters a list at the beginning of a play that tells who is in the play (Lesson 3)

cause-and-effect structure a text organization that shows what happens and why (Lesson 5)

character usually a person, but sometimes an animal or an object, in a story or a play (Lesson 1)

comparative adjective an adjective that compares two things using the ending -*er*—such as *bigger* or *faster*—or the word *more*—such as *more delicious* (Lesson 17)

comparative adverb an adverb that compares two actions using the ending -*er*—such as *earlier*—or the word *more*—such as *more quickly* (Lesson 17)

compare to show the similarities between plots, characters, settings, themes, or points of view (Lesson 4)

compare-and-contrast structure the text organization that tells how things or ideas are alike and different (Lesson 5)

complex sentence a sentence that includes a complete thought and an incomplete thought (Lesson 15)

compound sentence a sentence that has two or more simple sentences, usually connected by a comma (Lesson 15)

conclusion the end of a report or other piece of writing, in which the writer restates a topic or main idea (Lesson 15)

conflict a problem that the characters in a fictional narrative have to solve (Lesson 13)

conjunction a word, such as *and, or,* or *but,* that joins other words or groups of words (Lesson 11)

context clue the words or phrases around an unknown word that help the reader understand the meaning (Lesson 1)

contrast to show the differences between plots, characters, settings, themes, or points of view (Lesson 4)

cookbook a book that gives directions for how to make foods (Lesson 5)

coordinating conjunction a word, such as *and, or,* or *but*, that joins two or more words that are used in the same way (Lesson 17)

details information in a narrative or presentation that backs up the main idea or the opinion (Lesson 19)

diagram a drawing with labels that shows the parts of an object or how something works (Lesson 8)

dialogue the words that characters say in a story or play; a conversation between characters (Lesson 3)

dictionary a book that gives the meanings of many words (Lesson 18)

document an official paper about a law or an agreement (Lesson 7)

domain-specific vocabulary words that relate to a specific topic (Lesson 7)

drama a special kind of fiction story, often called a *play;* usually performed on a stage or in front of a camera (Lesson 3)

edit to correct mistakes in grammar, spelling, capitalization, and punctuation (Lesson 11)

events the things that happen in a story (Lesson 1)

evidence details that support a claim (Lesson 11)

fable a made-up story that teaches a lesson (Lesson 1)

fact a piece of information that can be proved (Lesson 5)

fiction stories made up by people (Lesson 1)

first draft the first time that something is written down (Lesson 11)

first-person point of view a way of telling a story in which the narrator is a character in the story and uses the pronouns *I, me,* and *my* (Lesson 2)

flowchart a chart or other graphic feature that shows the steps in a process (Lesson 8)

folktale a story that is told by people to other people over time (Lesson 1)

future tense the verb tense that shows what will happen (Lesson 12)

genre a kind of story, such as a fable or myth (Lesson 18)

glossary a list at the end of a text that gives the meanings of important terms in the text (Lesson 18)

graph a diagram that shows information in a visual way (Lesson 8)

graphic feature a diagram, map, or other visual aid that explains the text or gives extra information (Lesson 7)

heading a word or phrase that tells what a section of text is about (Lesson 5)

historical fiction a story that takes place in the past and may tell about important real events from history (Lesson 1)

hyperlink a word or phrase in online documents that you can click on to jump to a new Web page (Lesson 5)

illustration a drawing or other picture that shows what something looks like (Lesson 7)

informational text nonfiction text that informs readers about a topic (Lesson 5)

Internet the system of computer networks of facts, news, and opinions; also called the World Wide Web (Lesson 14)

key word a word that is important to a topic (Lesson 5)

label a short word or phrase that names something in a diagram, map, or other graphic aid (Lesson 15)

library a room or place that has books, magazines, encyclopedias, and other materials (Lesson 14)

lines rows of words; the basic structure of a poem (Lesson 2)

linking words and phrases words and phrases, such as *because, therefore,* and *for example,* that connect ideas and help them flow smoothly (Lesson 12)

literal language words or phrases that mean the same as what they mean (Lesson 2)

main idea the most important idea in a piece of writing or a presentation, usually stated at the beginning (Lesson 5)

map a drawing of an area of land or water (Lesson 7)

multiple-meaning words words that are spelled the same but have more than one meaning (Lesson 9)

myth a story that explains how things in nature came to be; can also tell how and why things work the way they do (Lesson 1)

narrative a story about real or made-up characters and events (Lesson 11)

narrator the character or person who tells a story (Lesson 1)

nonfiction writing that gives information about real people, real places, and real events (Lesson 5)

nonliteral language words and phrases that mean something different from their usual dictionary meanings (Lesson 2)

opinion a statement based on personal feelings (Lesson 6)

opinion piece a type of writing that states an opinion on a topic and gives reasons that readers should think the same way (Lesson 11)

past tense the verb tense that shows what happened before now, in the past (Lesson 12)

persuasive text nonfiction text that tries to make people do something or agree with an idea (Lesson 6)

photograph an actual picture of something or someone (Lesson 7)

plot the order of events, or things that happen, in a story (Lesson 1)

poetry a special type of writing that uses words in creative ways to describe things or show feelings; often written in stanzas, with rhyming lines; also called *poems* (Lesson 2)

point of view the outlook that someone has about the world or in a story; also called *perspective* (Lesson 1)

prefix an affix added to the beginning of a word that changes the word's meaning (Lesson 3)

present tense the verb tense that shows what is happening now, or in the present (Lesson 12)

presentation a talk or speech, usually to give information or to share an opinion (Lesson 19)

present-day fiction a story that takes place at the present time (Lesson 1)

prewriting choosing a topic and deciding what to say about it; the first step in the writing process (Lesson 11)

problem-and-solution structure the text organization in which an author gives facts about a problem and gives a possible solution (Lesson 6)

publish to let others read your work, either in print or digitally; the last step of the writing process (Lesson 11)

punctuation the marks that writers use in sentences to help explain meaning (Lesson 13)

purpose the reason for writing (Lesson 11)

real-life connection a connection between a word or phrase and the world (Lesson 5)

recount to remember and retell a story (Lesson 4)

report a nonfiction article that gives readers information (Lesson 15)

research to gather facts and information from sources such as books, Web sites, and newspapers (Lesson 14)

resolution the end of a story; how characters solve the story's problem (Lesson 11)

revise to make changes or corrections to a draft or piece of writing (Lesson 11)

rhyme the name for words on different lines that have the same ending sound (Lesson 2)

rhythm the "beat," or pattern of stressed and unstressed syllables, in lines of poetry (Lesson 2)

root word the base, or main part, of a word that tells the word's meaning (Lesson 3)

scene a section of a drama, smaller than an act (Lesson 3)

science fiction a story that tells about science, machines, and events in the future, and sometimes on other worlds (Lesson 1)

scientific text nonfiction text that tells readers about a science topic (Lesson 8)

sequence the order in which things happen (Lesson 5)

set in a drama or play, the way a scene looks to the audience (Lesson 3)

setting where and when a story takes place (Lesson 1)

shades of meaning a term for words that are related and have similar meanings (Lesson 2)

sidebar a short group of sentences or paragraphs next to an article that gives more information about a topic (Lesson 5)

simple sentence a sentence that has a subject and a verb and tells a complete thought (Lesson 15)

source a book, Web site, or other reference material that helps a writer find information (Lesson 14)

spatial text structure the text organization that organizes details by the space they take up; uses signal words like *top, middle,* and *bottom* (Lesson 8)

speaker the narrator of a poem (Lesson 2)

speech what someone says about a topic (Lesson 5)

stage directions the instructions in a drama, in italic type, that tell the actors what to do and tell about lighting and sound (Lesson 3)

stanza a group of lines that makes up a section of a poem (Lesson 2)

steps in a process a type of text organization that explains how to do something (Lesson 8)

subject-verb agreement when the subject and the verb of a sentence match in number as singular or plural (Lesson 16)

subordinating conjunction a word, such as *although, since,* or *because,* that connects a subordinate clause to the rest of a sentence (Lesson 17)

suffix an affix added to the end of a word that changes the word's meaning (Lesson 3)

summarize to retell the main points or plot of a text in your own words (Lesson 18)

summary a restatement of the main idea and the most important details (Lesson 9)

superlative adjective an adjective that compares more than two things using the ending -*est*—such as *nicest*—or the word *most*—such as *most delicious* (Lesson 17)

superlative adverb an adverb that compares more than two actions using the ending -*est*—such as *earliest*—or the word *most*—such as *most slowly* (Lesson 17)

supporting details important information about a main idea (Lesson 5)

table a graphic feature that shows information in columns and rows (Lesson 8)

technical text informative text that gives details about how something works or tells how to do something (Lesson 8)

text feature in a story or book, text such as a heading or caption that helps readers find information (Lesson 5)

text structure the way a text is organized, such as by sequence, cause and effect, or comparing and contrasting (Lesson 8)

textbook a book that gives facts and details about a topic (Lesson 5)

theme the important lesson or message in a story or play that the writer wants the reader or audience to learn (Lesson 1)

third-person point of view a way of telling a story in which the narrator is someone outside the story and uses the pronouns *he*, *she*, and *they* (Lesson 2)

timeline a graphic feature that shows the dates when important things happened (Lesson 7)

time-order word a word or phrase that tells when something happens and in what order, and how much time passes in between (Lesson 13)

topic the subject of a text (Lesson 11)

topic sentence a sentence, early in a paragraph, article, or report, that states the main idea (Lesson 15)

verb a word that shows action or a state of being (Lesson 12)

verb tense the form of a verb that shows when an action happens (Lesson 12)

visual aid see *graphic feature*

writing getting ideas down on paper or using a computer; the second step in the writing process (Lesson 11)

NOTES